LORD
CURZON
1859-1925
A Bibliography

LORD CURZON 1859–1925

A Bibliography

James G. Parker

BIBLIOGRAPHIES OF BRITISH STATESMEN, NO. 5

GREGORY PALMER, SERIES EDITOR

Greenwood Press

New York • Westport, Connecticut • London

Library of Congress Cataloging-in-Publication Data

Parker, James G.
    Lord Curzon, 1859–1925 : a bibliography / James G. Parker.
       p. cm.—(Bibliographies of British statesmen, ISSN
  1056–5515 ; no. 5)
    Includes indexes.
    ISBN 0–313–28122–X (alk. paper)
    1. Curzon, George Nathaniel Curzon, Marquis of, 1859–1925—
  Bibliography. I. Title. II. Series.
  Z8206.58.P37   1991
  [DA565.C95]
  016.95403′55′092—dc20   91–9473

British Library Cataloguing in Publication Data is available.

Library of Congress Catalog Card Number: 91–9473
ISBN: 0–313–28122–X
ISSN: 1056–5515

First published in 1991

Greenwood Press, 88 Post Road West, Westport, CT 06881
An imprint of Greenwood Publishing Group, Inc.

Printed in the United States of America

The paper used in this book complies with the
Permanent Paper Standard issued by the National
Information Standards Organization (Z39.48–1984).

10 9 8 7 6 5 4 3 2 1

The author and publisher gratefully acknowledge the National Portrait Gallery,
London, for permission to reproduce a portrait of Lord Curzon.

Contents

Preface

The compilation of a bibliography of manuscript, printed, and other sources relating to the life and career of George Curzon has proved a daunting task. There can be few figures in modern British public life who have achieved distinction in such a wide range of fields. He is now best remembered for his viceroyalty which epitomized British power in India at its height in the late Victorian period. To contemporaries, however, George Curzon was equally well known as explorer and travel writer, orator, preserver of Britain's and India's architectural heritages, chancellor of Oxford University, and post-war foreign secretary.

His viceroyalty or foreign secretaryship would each alone justify separate bibliographical treatment if account were to be taken of every published book or collection of papers touching on his contribution to the history of British India or British foreign policy in these two crucial periods. To encompass both of these, as well as the many other aspects of Curzon's career, the section below covering biographical and historical studies confines itself on the whole to works devoted to him or those that make a substantial or original contribution to our understanding of his personal role in issues and events. Some additional works have also been included where they provide useful background to some aspect of his career.

Likewise, only significant groups of Curzon's private correspondence with contemporaries have been included in the section on manuscript sources, no attempt being made to document every surviving letter or letters from him, or every reference to him among the papers of others. The official records covered are those relating to the Cabinet and the departments of state in which Curzon held office. No attempt has been made to identify relevant material among the extensive records of other departments with which Curzon had dealings as viceroy or government minister.

Every effort has been made to provide full bibliographical details for published and unpublished works cited and to give some indication of their subject matter. It has not been possible to locate copies of some works and in these cases entries are limited to whatever details were available. In a few cases the title of a work is self-explanatory and requires no further explanation. Given the range of Curzon's interests and the diversity of issues with which he was involved in public office, omissions will inevitably have occurred and opinion will differ among specialists over the most appropriate material for inclusion in a study of this kind. It is hoped, however, that the present bibliography will bring together for the first time a full range of sources for the career of this fascinating and multifaceted man.

LORD CURZON 1859-1925
A Bibliography

George Curzon, Marquess of Kedleston, 1914, by J. Cooke after John Singer Sargent. Reprinted courtesy of the National Portrait Gallery, London.

I. Biographical Essay

George Nathaniel Curzon was born on January 11, 1859, the eldest son and heir of the fourth Baron Scarsdale. His early education was conducted at Kedleston, his family's Derbyshire seat, and at private school before he was sent to the public school, Eton College, in 1872. At Eton he demonstrated a precocious talent for public speaking and writing and became president of the College's famous literary society. He was greatly influenced by Oscar Browning, at the height of his reputation as a College master, and he remained a life-long friend of Browning's. During this formative period of his education the seeds of his later fascination with India and the East seem to have been sown. It was at Eton too that the curvature of his spine which was to dominate and inhibit his adult life so much, forcing him to wear an iron corset, first manifested itself.

Curzon went up to Balliol College, Oxford, in 1872. Here the self-assurance of his writing and oratory, his capacity for long periods of intense mental effort, and a remarkable facility for assimilating great masses of detail marked him out to contemporaries as being destined for great things. It was to a career in politics that he was attracted, and he confidently looked forward to achieving the highest political office. His inclinations were to the Conservative party but he was no slavish adherent to traditional Tory views. He revitalized and dominated the university's Canning Club and soon after leaving Oxford was contributing articles to journals on the need for a more radical form of Conservatism.

He entered Parliament in 1886 as Conservative member for the Southport division of Lancashire. Over the next nine years domestic politics assumed second place to a program of extensive travel which took him around the world twice and, despite his physical disability, through some of the most rugged and often unexplored terrain of Central Asia. He established himself as a leading authority on the geography, culture, and politics of Asia and the East. He was in great demand by the national journals and reviews of the period for accounts of his travels and his political views. In addition to a number of books he supplemented his relatively restricted personal income by contributing more than sixty articles to newspapers and periodicals in the years down to 1898. His travels reinforced his belief in Britain's imperial role abroad and convinced him that Russia represented the greatest single threat to the British empire in India.

His marriage in 1895 to Mary Leiter, daughter of the Chicago millionaire Levi Leiter, put his personal financial position on a more secure footing. Her charm and unselfishness were the ideal foil for what seemed to many an aloofness and coldness in Curzon's makeup. In the following years he enhanced his growing political reputation as under-secretary at the India Office under Lord Cross and at the Foreign Office under Lord Salisbury, and at the same time, with his wife, became better known to the public as a society figure. The Curzons were prominent members of the aristocratic literary and social circle known as the Souls. It came, then, as no great surprise to close friends when Curzon was chosen to succeed Lord Elgin as viceroy of India in 1898. For Curzon it was the realization of an ambition nurtured since his school days and brought steadily to fruition by travel, writing, and political office.

The early years of Curzon's viceroyalty were characterized by attempts to streamline the slow-moving and cumbersome bureaucracy of Indian government. He set in motion reviews of education and land assessment policies, and created a North West Frontier Province from part of the Punjab in the face of strong opposition from the Indian Civil Service. At the same time, however, resistance was tempered by respect as both Indian and British observers recognized the sincerity of his aims, his industry, and his willingness to learn.

The great Durbar of 1903 to celebrate the accession of Edward VII marked the high point of Curzon's viceroyalty. There had already been indications in the previous year of the difficulties to come between him and the India Office in London over the cost of the Durbar and his insistence on marking the event by some form of tax remission for India. Although his great works of reform— railways, irrigation, famine relief, archaeological surveys—continued, relations with the secretary of state in London were further aggravated by what was felt to be an over-aggressive foreign policy in Afghanistan and Tibet. Inevitably the Cabinet too became involved over Curzon's refusal to fund the whole cost of the Indian forces fighting with the British Army in South Africa from Indian revenues. Among Indians, also, the respect he had engendered by his reforming zeal became somewhat diminished as his absolute opposition to making any concessions to demands for Indian self-government became known and by his decision (implemented after his departure) to divide Bengal into two separate administrative units. The decision was widely interpreted in India as an attempt to punish the middle classes for their support of the nationalist movement.

After a brief spell in England in 1904, Curzon returned for a second term of office. His remaining year, however, was to be dominated by dissension within the government of India, especially friction between him and his commander-in-chief, Lord Kitchener, over the latter's constitutional position. The dispute arose over the system of "dual control" of the Indian Army whereby responsibility for many matters of a purely administrative nature lay with the military member of the viceroy's council and not with the commander-in-chief. Kitchener's proposals that the commander-in-chief should have control of every aspect of military affairs was opposed by Curzon. After a protracted struggle, in which the India Office in London became involved, a compromise solution was suggested by Curzon and agreed upon. However, when the appointment of a new military member was made from London without consultation with the viceroy, Curzon offered his resignation, which was accepted. Curzon returned to England in November 1905 feeling disillusioned and betrayed by a government he felt he had served faithfully and in which his friends of long standing, Balfour and Brodrick, served as prime minister and Indian secretary.

After his return his sense of duty and a wish to avoid recriminations prevented him from attempting to justify his position publicly. He was not to hold government office again until 1915. In the intervening years he devoted himself to his duties as chancellor of Oxford University (from 1907) and to other interests such as the Royal Geographical Society (of which he was president 1911–14, and the purchase and restoration of historic buildings such as Bodiam Castle in Sussex and Tattershall Castle in Lincolnshire. Gradually, however, as can be seen by his speeches and the letters he wrote to *The Times*, he came to terms with his Indian disappointments and with the death of Lady Curzon in 1906. He began to involve himself in political issues on which he had strong views, such as the national service movement (which he supported) or women's suffrage and Irish home rule (which he opposed).

He re-entered Parliament in 1908 by virtue of his Irish peerage, and by the time of the constitutional crisis of 1910–11 was a leading figure on the Opposition benches in the House of Lords. Return to public office came in 1915 with an invitation to join Asquith's coalition government as lord privy seal, but he was excluded from the War Cabinet until July of the following year. Under Lloyd George he was given more scope for his administrative talents by being put in charge of the Shipping Control Committee and then the newly formed Air Board. He threw himself into both with his accustomed energy and commitment.

With the end of the war and the departure of Lloyd George and Balfour, then foreign secretary, to the Paris peace conference, Curzon was put in temporary charge of foreign affairs in January 1919. He set in motion negotiations with Persia to enable the withdrawal of the Allied occupation force without relinquishing British influence. A mission under Lord Milner was dispatched to Egypt to consider what, if any, concessions might be made to self-government while preserving the country's protectorate status. The latter initiative was to prove more successful than the former, and an Egyptian government under Sarwat Pasha was accepted by Britain in 1922.

Of more immediate urgency for Curzon when he succeeded Balfour as foreign secretary at the end of 1919 was the need to come to some decision over the future of Turkey, Germany's defeated partner, in the face of Greek claims to lands in Asia Minor; the emergence of the Kemalist movement in Turkey; and the jealousies of the Allies. Curzon's principal object was the protection of the Straits which he hoped to achieve by depriving Turkey of Constantinople and her European territory. This was a departure from Britain's traditional policy of supporting the "sick man" and was not in alignment with the more pro-Turkish stance of France. Curzon's task of finding a middle path to accommodate the disparate aims of the Allies was further complicated by the independent line taken by Lloyd George who was an outspoken supporter of Greek claims. The ensuing decline in Anglo-French relations precipitated the Chanak crisis of November 1922 when the French withdrew their contingent of the Allied peace-keeping force from the Dardanelles. The general election that followed resulted in the replacement of the coalition government by a Conservative administration under Bonar Law in which Curzon retained his foreign affairs portfolio. The Turko-Greek question culminated in a personal success for Curzon at the Conference of Lausanne. Although the conference broke up with no overall agreement, Curzon impressed all parties by his detailed background knowledge of the main issues and the firmness of his resolve.

Among the many other questions of post-war diplomacy in which he found himself involved, the most important in terms of Anglo-French relations was the matter of German reparations to the Allies for war damage and loss. Curzon fought hard to reconcile the claims of the French and the Belgians with the ability of the Germans to pay. Eventually, through Curzon's efforts, the French were persuaded to accept an independent inquiry which eventually produced the Dawes plan.

Curzon experienced mixed success as foreign secretary. His touch was surest in matters affecting Asia and the East, but even here his old-fashioned imperialism, late-Victorian training under Salisbury, and lack of sympathy for nationalism left him out of step with the realities of the post-war world and Britain's much-reduced standing in it. Within the Foreign Office, too, he failed to make his mark and win the confidence of his staff. He was unable to restore the Foreign Office's position in foreign policy-making. Lloyd George, who had a poor opinion of diplomats, preferred to conduct his own negotiations or, as in the matter of reparations, to work through the Cabinet Office, War Office, and the Treasury.

In the autumn of 1923 Baldwin called an election on the issue of Protection and was defeated. When the Tories returned to office in 1924 Curzon was not invited to resume at the Foreign Office. His heart was no longer in ministerial office. In May of that year Law had resigned the premiership on grounds of ill health. After three decades of public service Curzon felt his hour had finally come. It was Baldwin, however, who was summoned to the Palace and asked to form a government, denying Curzon the reward he felt was his by right. Despite his intense bitterness and disappointment at the King's decision, his sense of duty obliged him to accept the lord presidency under Baldwin in November and he held this office until his death in March 1925.

II. Chronology

1919–24	foreign secretary
1921	created Marquess Curzon of Kedleston
1924–25	lord president of the council; leader of the House of Lords
1925	death

III. Manuscript Sources

A. PUBLISHED GUIDES

1. Private Papers

1.   Cook, Chris. *Sources in British political history 1900–1951. Volume 1. A guide to the archives of selected organisations and societies.* London: British Library of Political and Economic Science, 1975. 330.

Guide to surviving records and other source materials for political parties, trade unions, pressure groups, and other organizations with some form of political involvement. These include bodies of relevance to Curzon's career such as the National League for Opposing Women's Suffrage, the various groups concerned with Indian self-government, and with the national service movement before and during the Great War.

2.   ———. *Sources in British political history 1900–1951. Volume 2. A guide to the private papers of selected public servants.* London: British Library of Political and Economic Science, 1975. 297.

Includes entries for some 1,500 senior public servants active in British public life in this period. These comprise diplomats, civil servants, colonial administrators, and military commanders. Many were colleagues of Curzon in India or the Foreign Office and diplomatic service, including Sir Walter Lawrence and Kitchener.

3.   ———. *Sources in British political history 1900–1951. Volumes 3 and 4. A guide to the private papers of members of Parliament.* London: British Library of Political and Economic Science, 1977. 281 and 272.

Provides summary descriptions of the papers of Curzon himself and fellow members of the House of Commons in this period.

4. Cook, Chris and Jeffrey Weeks. *Sources in British political history 1900–1951. Volume 5. A Guide to the papers of selected writers and intellectuals and publishers*. London: British Library of Political and Economic Science, 1978. 221.

Describes papers of newspaper proprietors, journalists, editors, political theorists, academics, businessmen, publicists, and others. Among those with connections with Curzon are Gertrude Bell, Sir Valentine Chirol, Geoffrey Dawson, Ralph Deakin, and Oscar Browning.

5. Cook, Chris. *Sources in British political history 1900–1951. Volume 6. First consolidated supplement*. London: British Library of Political and Economic Science, 1985. 272.

Supplement to Cook's five previous volumes noting changes in locations, and new groups, of papers for existing entries, as well as individuals and organizations not hitherto included.

6. Hazlehurst, Cameron and Christine Woodland. *A guide to the papers of British Cabinet ministers 1900–1951*. London: Royal Historical Society, 1974. 174.

Provides a summary of the main groups of Curzon's papers, as well as those of colleagues in government.

7. Royal Commission on Historical Manuscripts. *Guides to sources for British history 1. Papers of British Cabinet ministers 1782–1900*. London: HMSO, 1982. 75.

Brings together information about the nature and location of the private papers of more than 200 Cabinet ministers, including Lords Cross and Salisbury, under whom Curzon served at the India and Foreign Offices.

8. ———. *Guides to sources for British history 4. Private papers of British diplomats 1782–1900*. London: HMSO, 1985. 80.

Includes a summary of Curzon's own papers as under-secretary at the Foreign Office as well as those of Lord Salisbury and senior British diplomats abroad in this period.

9. ———. *Guides to sources for British history 5. Private papers of British colonial governors 1782–1900*. London: HMSO, 1986. 66.

Includes papers of a number of administrators in Canada, South Africa, Ceylon, and the Far East with whom Curzon dealt as viceroy.

10. ———. *Guides to sources for British history 6. Private papers of British politicians 1782–1900*. London: HMSO, 1989.

Describes the papers of more than 700 men and women active in British political life 1782–1900, including M.P.s, journalists, private secretaries, political hostesses, and others. Among those who had close connections with Curzon were W. Scawen Blunt, St. John Brodrick, Oscar Browning, George Wyndham, the 10th Earl of Wemyss and 2nd Earl of Selborne.

2. Official Papers

11. Farrington, Anthony. *Guide to the records of the India Office military department*. London: India Office Library and Records, 1982. 513.

Includes material for the period of the "dual control" controversy and references to Sir E.G. Barrow, Kitchener, etc.

12. Moir, Martin. *A general guide to the India Office Records*. London: British Library, 1988. 331.

Overview of the official papers in the India Office Library and Records with a descriptive inventory of every class of records. Private papers are not described.

13. Public Record Office. *List of Cabinet Office papers 1880–1914*. PRO handbooks No. 4. London: HMSO, 1964. 143.

Provides details of papers felt by Cabinet ministers to be sufficiently important to be printed and circulated to other Cabinet members. After 1916 this was conducted by the Cabinet Office secretariat, but copies of earlier papers are to be found only among the private papers of ministers. Included in the present volume are papers for the period of Curzon's viceroyalty in Persia, proposals for remitting taxation at the Delhi Durbar, the Tibetan expedition, relations with Afghanistan, and French activity in Siam. A number of the papers are memoranda or notes by Curzon for the Cabinet's consideration.

14. ———. *List of Cabinet Office papers 1915 and 1916*. PRO handbooks No. 9. London: HMSO, 1966. 112.

Takes the papers described in the volume above up to 1916. These include items dealing with the Dardanelles campaign, national service, and the defense of India, with all of which Curzon was involved in this period.

15. ———. *List of papers of the Committee of Imperial Defence to 1914*. London: HMSO, 1964. 46.

Provides details of the records of the committee of which Curzon was a member and, from 1924, chairman. There is extensive material also for the period of his viceroyalty relating to Indian defense, Russian activity on the North-West Frontier, and other Indian issues.

16. ———. *The records of the Cabinet Office to 1922*. PRO handbooks No. 11. London: HMSO, 1966. 52.

Provides guidelines for using the records of the Cabinet Office and historical background on the workings of the Office.

17. ———. *The records of the Foreign Office 1782–1939*. PRO handbooks No. 13. London: HMSO, 1969. 180.

Guide to the official records of the Foreign Office and to the private papers of diplomats and foreign secretaries held by the Public Record Office, with background on the nature of paper keeping and filing in the Foreign Office in this period.

18.   Tuson, Penelope. *The records of the British residency and agencies in the Persian Gulf*. London: India Office Library and Records, 1979. 201.

Describes the surviving correspondence and papers of the British agencies in the Gulf 1763–1947 as well as other related Gulf materials among the India Office records.

3. General Sources

19.   Hall, Lesley. *A brief guide to sources for the study of Afghanistan in the India Office Records*. London: India Office Library and Records, 1981. 60.

Surveys the sources for Afghanistan, including a section for Curzon's viceroyalty when Abdur Rahman Khan was amir.

20.   Hartley, Janet M. *Guide to documents and manuscripts in the United Kingdom relating to Russia and the Soviet Union*. London and New York: Mansell, 1987. 526.

Surveys material held by some 300 bodies in this country and includes sources for Anglo-Russian relations over Afghanistan, Persia, etc., as well as for Curzon's foreign secretaryship, including the proposed trade agreement of 1921 and Allied intervention in the Russian civil war.

21.   Jones, Philip. *Britain and Palestine 1914–1948. Archival sources for the history of the British mandate*. Oxford: Oxford University Press, 1979. 246.

Notes records of organizations, societies, and individuals, including Curzon, Balfour, etc., with a bearing on the history of Palestine.

22.   Pearson, J. D. *A guide to western manuscripts and documents in the British Isles relating to south and southeast Asia. Volume 1. London*. London and New York: Mansell, 1989.

Update of Wainwright and Matthews (no. 24 below), but including the holdings of the India Office Library and Records omitted from the earlier survey.

22a.   Singh, Amar Kaur Jasbir. *A guide to source materials in the India Office Library and Records for the history of Tibet, Sikkim and Bhutan 1765–1950*. London: British Library, 1988. 187.

Covers official records and private papers, including material on Curzon's relations with these states and the Younghusband expedition.

23.   Thomas, Timothy N. *Indians overseas. A guide to source materials in the India Office records for the study of Indian emigration*. London: British Library, 1985. 97.

Describes sources for the history of Indian emigration, mainly the indentured labor system. Some light is thrown on Curzon's opposition to the system which he regarded as producing "slaves of empire."

24. Wainwright, M. D. and Noel Matthews. *A guide to western manuscripts and documents in the British Isles relating to south and south east Asia.* London: Oxford University Press, 1965. 532. (See also no. 22 above.)

Wide-ranging survey of material relating to India and the rest of south and south-east Asia including much for Curzon's period as viceroy. The volume covers official and private papers, but excludes the holdings of the India Office Library and Records.

B. PRIVATE PAPERS

The following groups of private papers of Curzon, members of his family, and contemporaries are based largely on the information available in the Historical Manuscripts Commission's National Register of Archives and its Personal Index. This index is selective and only significant collections of correspondence and papers with some bearing on Curzon's life have been included. Where a catalogue of the papers described is available in the National Register of Archives its numerical reference in the NRA (in the form "NRA 23456") has been given. These lists and the NRA's Personal Index can be consulted in the Commission's search room in Quality House, Quality Court, Chancery Lane, London WC2A 1HP.

1. Curzon

The bulk of Curzon's private papers are held by the India Office Library and Records where they constitute the largest single private collection (MSS. Eur. F111–12). That so much has survived is in great measure due to his insistence on involving himself in the minutiae of every aspect of his official and private life, and to his reluctance to throw anything away. The main exceptions are his papers as Chancellor of Oxford University, most of which seem to have become detached from the main archive and can now no longer be traced, and his correspondence as president of the National League for Opposing Women's Suffrage which, uncharacteristically, he destroyed in 1919 "since it would never interest anyone and the cause has been lost" (MSS. Eur. F112/807). Curzon seldom employed a secretary, preferring to write his own letters. He kept few copies of these and, as a result, the correspondence in the collection is largely incoming.

25. Early correspondence with friends, school and university teachers, "Souls," and others 1869–1903, including St. John Brodrick, Benjamin Jowett, Oscar Browning, and Cecil Spring Rice; notebooks, MSS. of essays, speeches, and other papers relating to his years at Eton and Oxford 1866–84, including reminiscences of his early life; notebooks, correspondence, press cuttings, photographs, etc., relating to his travels 1880–1903; a few letters and papers as under-secretary for India, mainly on his appointment and concerning opium and railways; miscellaneous correspondence and papers as under-secretary for foreign affairs, including letters from Lord Salisbury and material on slavery, the Paris Exhibition 1900, and a visit by the Empress of Russia 1896; some letters and papers concerning his parliamentary campaigns in south Derbyshire and Southport 1882–95; printed Foreign Office and India Office papers, including reports of the Afghan Boundary Commission 1888–89 and official correspondence with Burma, China, Persia, etc.

Semi-official correspondence as viceroy with Queen Victoria and King Edward VII 1898–1904 (printed), with Lord George Hamilton, St. John Brodrick, Sir Arthur Godley, Arthur Balfour, Lord Lansdowne, and others, with individuals in India and with the Amir of Afghanistan 1899–1905 (MS., typescript and printed); private correspondence with Cabinet ministers, India Office officials, and others 1898–1907, including Balfour, Brodrick, Lord Elgin, and Sir Walter Lawrence; private correspondence on particular subjects, including his Irish peerage, 1898–1908; official correspondence and papers on internal Indian administration, including the army, education, relations with independent princes, archaeology and indentured labor in South Africa; official papers relating to Indian foreign policy, mainly relations with Afghanistan, China and the Far East, Persia, Russia, and Tibet; correspondence and papers concerning the "dual control" controversy, including letters from Lord Kitchener, minutes by Curzon and Kitchener, related press cuttings, and notes by Curzon on his difficulties in India 1888–1916; letters and telegrams received after his resignation 1905; correspondence and papers relating to his interests after 1905, including the Victoria Memorial Hall in Calcutta, the removal of the Indian capital to Delhi and the Indian nationalist movement 1909–23; printed "summaries" of his Indian administration, including public works, land revenue, railways, and foreign affairs; official papers relating to internal and foreign affairs and army matters; abstracts of proceedings of the viceroy's council 1904–10; speeches 1898–1901 (printed); official Government of India publications relating to archaeology, censuses, the Delhi Durbar, etc.

General correspondence 1906–15 (arranged alphabetically); some correspondence and papers as chancellor of Oxford University, mainly relating to constitutional reform 1907–20 and including a draft of his Principles and practice of university reform; correspondence and papers relating to other honorary offices, including his work for the Clive Memorial Fund, Royal Geographical Society and National Gallery 1904–25; some surviving correspondence concerning women's suffrage, including a note by him on the destruction of his other papers on this subject, 1910–18; correspondence and papers on foreign affairs, including Persia and Tibet, 1905–19, and on home affairs, including the constitutional crisis 1910–11 and the National Service League 1908–14; personal correspondence and papers 1904–34, including material concerning his peerages 1904–11, his motor accident 1906–10, and an autobiographical note 1910.

First World War letters and papers, including Cabinet notes from 1915, Cabinet and War Council papers 1914–18 (mainly from 1916), committee reports by him, papers relating to the formation of the Lloyd George administration in December 1916, confidential and unprinted minutes of War Cabinet meetings, papers on the Dardanelles landings, the Mesopotamian campaign, conscription, and conscientious objection; a few papers concerning the Air Board and Shipping Control Committee 1915–17; correspondence and papers relating to the Irish rising 1916 and foreign affairs 1916–19; some letters and related material on his leadership of the House of Lords, mainly concerning honors and formal occasions, 1916–25; diaries (3 vols.) of his visits to the Western Front 1916, 1918.

Foreign Office private correspondence with British ambassadors to France (Lords Derby, Hardinge, and Crewe), from Lord d'Abernon on his visit to Warsaw 1920 (with his Berlin diary 1921–23), from Sir Auckland Geddes, British ambassador to the U.S.A., 1920–21, and extensive other correspondence with diplomats, civil servants, politicians, etc., 1919–25; correspondence and papers arranged by country or region, including Europe (reparations, proposed Channel tunnel) and north Africa, Egypt, Syria, Palestine, Turkey, and the Middle East; correspondence and papers concerning the Imperial Conferences 1921, 1923, and the Lausanne Peace Conference 1922–23; papers on domestic and miscellaneous affairs, including his notes of Cabinet meetings 1920–24 and the selection of Baldwin as prime minister May 1923.

Correspondence with members of the British and European royal families 1899–1924, including letters from Edward VII 1899–1909, George V 1903–5, 1921, and Edward VIII 1918–21.

Scrapbooks and press cuttings relating to home affairs, India, etc.

MSS., drafts, etc. of his works, with related correspondence concerning their publication, working papers, press cuttings, including much for "On the Indian frontier" which Curzon was prevented from publishing following his appointment as viceroy.

Correspondence and papers relating to his marriages to Mary Leiter (including letters from his father and Levi Leiter) 1887–98, and to Grace Curzon 1912–20; letters to him from Grace Curzon 1915–24; papers relating to his investments, household expenses, etc.; papers relating to his properties, mainly Hackwood Park, Tattershall Castle, Montacute House, and Kedleston, including letters concerning their restoration; posthumous papers, including correspondence relating to Lord Ronaldshay's *Life* 1925–31; papers of other members of his family, including letters from him to his mother and father 1867–1915, to Grace, Lady Curzon 1916–25 with other of her papers 1916–54; photograph albums, mainly relating to India.

India Office Library and Records, London (MSS. Eur. F111–12). NRA 20536.

26.   Correspondence as under-secretary for foreign affairs 1895–98 (2 vols.); correspondence of Curzon, Sir James Fergusson and J.W. Lowther as under-secretaries 1886–97 (1 vol.); correspondence as foreign secretary 1919–24 (10 vols.), including 3 volumes relating to Yugoslavia, Turkey, the United States, etc.

Public Record Office, Kew, Surrey (FO 800/28, 147–58). NRA 23627.

27. Letters (50) from Lord Carmichael, Sir William Foster, B.A. Gupte, Lord Minto, and others on the Victorian Memorial Hall 1912–26.
University of Alberta Library, Edmonton (MS. Coll. Box 96/88). NRA 26023.

28. Correspondence (36 items) with Sir Henry Cotton and others relating to paintings and sculptures for the Victoria Memorial Hall 1895.
William R. Perkins Library, Duke University, Durham, North Carolina. NRA 25900.

29. Address to the electors of Southport June 1886; copies of his published speeches on general political matters 1891 and on fisheries 1892; collection of press cuttings and cartoons relating to Curzon.
Southport Public Library, Lancashire (Refs.: 942.725a, 825.915, 629.2Sa [Pamph.], B.20.S).

29a. Bodiam Castle deeds and manorial records 1599–1922.
East Sussex Record Office, Lewes (AMS 5691, 5981). NRA 23345.

30. Correspondence and papers relating to Tattershall Castle, including letters on his recovery of the castle mantelpieces 1911–12; correspondence with builders and craftsmen relating to the castle's restoration 1912–22; plans, building accounts, photographs, Curzon's notes on fabrics, etc., 1911–25 (2 vols. and c.300 items in all).
Lincolnshire Archives Office, Lincoln (NT/1–5). NRA 19642.

2. Curzon Family, Barons Scarsdale

30a. Solicitors' papers, including estate and manorial records, deeds, and Derbyshire Canal Company papers 17th–19th century.
Derbyshire Record Office, Matlock (Acc. 434). NRA 22676.

30b. Deeds, legal, family, estate, and household papers 12th–20th century, including some formal papers of Curzon relating to his appointments as viceroy and chancellor of Oxford University.
Viscount Scarsdale, Kedleston Hall, Derbyshire. NRA 1167.

3. Leiter Family

Curzon (née Leiter), Mary Victoria, Baroness Curzon (1870–1904).

31. Correspondence with Curzon and members of her family, journals, and diaries (50 vols.).
Lady Alexandra Metcalfe.

Leiter, Levi Zeigler (1834–1904), father of the above.

32. Correspondence, cashbooks, rentals, journals, insurance papers, trustees' minutes, and other records relating to the administration of his estate, including

correspondence of his daughters Daisy, Countess of Suffolk and Nancy Campbell, Joseph Leiter and Curzon, papers concerning Curzon's legal proceedings
against Joseph Leiter for mismanagement of the estate, records relating to the
estate's properties in Chicago, Wyoming, and the company town of Zeigler,
Illinois 1858–1965.

Chicago Historical Society Library, Illinois. See *National Union Catalog* MS
75–408.

4. Contemporaries

Asquith, Herbert Henry, 1st Earl of Oxford and Asquith (1852–1928).
Home secretary 1892–95; chancellor of the exchequer 1905–8; prime
minister 1908–16.

33. Letters (9) from Curzon to Asquith and his private secretary 1908–16;
memoranda by Curzon and Morley opposing the appointment of Kitchener as
viceroy of India 1910; letters (2) from Curzon 1915, including one on the
composition of the War Committee; correspondence of Asquith with Curzon,
Lloyd George, Balfour, and others on the resignation of Asquith's government
1916; miscellaneous letters from Curzon 1918, 1925.

Bodleian Library, Oxford University (MSS. Asquith vols. 11–35 passim).
NRA 12685.

Asquith, Emma Alice Margaret (Margot), Countess of Oxford and As-
quith (1864–1945).

34. Correspondence with Curzon.
Mark Bonham Carter Esq. See Kenneth Rose, *Superior person . . .* (No. 303
below).

Astor, Nancy Witcher, Viscountess Astor (1879–1964). Conservative
M.P. for Plymouth 1919–45.

35. Correspondence with politicians, literary figures, and others, including
letters (103) of a personal, social, etc. nature from Curzon 1909–20 and undated.
Reading University Library, Berkshire (MS. 1416, Curzon letters: 1416/1/4/
36–9).

Barnes, Sir Hugh Shakespear (1853–1940). Foreign secretary to the
government of India 1900–3; president of the central committee for the
Delhi Durbar 1903; lieutenant-governor of Burma 1903–5.

36. Correspondence, memoranda, and dispatches relating to the North-West
Frontier 1880–1908, including a copy of a letter from Curzon 1899; correspondence and papers on the Nushki railway 1899–1922, including copies of his letters
to Curzon 1917–18, 1922; other papers relating to India and Burma, including

the Burma Railway Co. 1902–4, Burmah Oil Co. 1904, and the separation of Burma and India 1905.

Bodleian Library, Oxford University (MSS. Eng. hist. C253–61).

Barrow, General Sir Edmund (1852–1934). Secretary to the military department of the government of India 1901–3; commander of the 1st. Peshawar Division 1904–7; proposed by Curzon (but not appointed) as military member of the viceroy's council.

37. Papers, including material relating to troop dispositions on the NW Frontier c. 1904–7, Indian Army reorganization and administration 1888–1919, and his criticisms of Kitchener's "dual control" proposals; diaries 1904–5; MS. and typescript autobiography, with related press cuttings, including much on his involvement in the Curzon-Kitchener controversy; correspondence with Curzon, Kitchener, Balfour, Brodrick, and others on this and other military matters 1903–6.

India Office Library and Records, London (MSS. Eur. E420). NRA 27513.

Birdwood, Field-Marshal Sir William Riddell, 1st Baron Birdwood of Anzac and Totnes (1865–1951). Military secretary to Lord Kitchener 1900–9; secretary to the military department of the government of India and member of the viceroy's council 1912–14.

38. Papers of Lord Kitchener (acquired by Birdwood as his military secretary): correspondence between Kitchener and Curzon, memoranda, minutes, etc., relating to Indian military affairs 1903–5, including the "dual control" dispute; also material on British relations with Afghanistan and Russian involvement there; correspondence of Kitchener and Lord Roberts on Indian Army reform 1903–4; further papers on "dual control" and army matters 1888–1914, including memoranda by Curzon and others, a note by Kitchener of an interview with Curzon on the proposed appointment of Sir Edmund Barrow as military member of the viceroy's council, a memorandum by Sir Beauchamp Duff ("Lord Curzon's proposed attack on the secretary of state in connection with the abolition of the military supply department . . ."), and correspondence among Curzon, Kitchener, and Balfour on Afghanistan, the Indian Defence Committee, etc.

Correspondence and papers of Birdwood 1900–17 relating to S. Africa, India, and the First World War, including letters to him from Kitchener and the India Office on dual control 1904–5.

India Office Library and Records, London (MSS. Eur. D686). NRA 27457.

Brodrick, (William) St. John Fremantle, 1st Earl of Midleton (1856–1942). Under-secretary for foreign affairs 1898–1900; secretary for war 1900–3; secretary for India 1903–5.

39. Papers as Indian secretary 1903–5, including correspondence with Curzon, Kitchener, Roberts, and George Wyndham on Afghanistan, Tibet, membership of the viceroy's council, etc., and with Kitchener and Balfour concerning the former's "dual control" dispute with Curzon; memoranda and booklets on Curzon's viceroyalty; correspondence with Curzon and others relating to the constitutional crisis 1911, to the First World War, and to Ireland 1917–20 including letters from Curzon and Lloyd George opposing the government policy of placating Sinn Fein 1917.

Public Record Office, Kew, Surrey (PRO 30/67). NRA 23461.

40. Correspondence as Indian secretary with Curzon 1903–6 (6 vols.). British Library, London (Add. MSS. 50072–7).

Browning, Oscar (1837–1923). Historian and Eton College master.

41. Letters (c. 170) from Curzon 1873–1912 on personal matters, India, etc. King's College Library, Cambridge University (MSS. 445–9). NRA 21235.

Cecil, Edgar Algernon Robert Gascoyne, Viscount Cecil of Chelwood (1864–1958). Under-secretary for foreign affairs 1915–18; minister of blockade 1916–18; assistant foreign secretary 1918–19; attended Paris Peace Conference 1919; S. African representative at the League of Nations 1920–22; lord privy seal 1923; chancellor of the Duchy of Lancaster 1924–27.

42. Special correspondence with Curzon 1910–24, Balfour, Asquith, and other political figures 1906–52; miscellaneous correspondence 1915–34 relating to foreign affairs; further special correspondence, including Foreign Office telegrams 1918–30, memoranda 1920–39; diaries and journals relating to League of Nations affairs 1917–37; general correspondence 1904–53; literary MSS. and correspondence c.1912–49.

British Library, London (Add. MSS. 51071–204).

43. Foreign Office correspondence and papers relating to the Balkans, Belgium, France, the Netherlands, Scandinavia, the United States, etc.; miscellaneous correspondence of Cecil and other under-secretaries 1915–19.

Public Record Office, Kew, Surrey (FO 800/195–8).

Cecil, Robert Arthur Talbot Gascoyne, 3rd Marquess of Salisbury (1830–1903). Foreign secretary 1878–80, 1885–92, 1895–1900; prime minister 1885–92, 1895–1902; lord privy seal 1900–02.

44. Papers as foreign secretary 1878–1900: includes correspondence with Queen Victoria, Cabinet colleagues, and others with occasional references to Curzon's work as under-secretary 1895–98 including his role as Foreign Office spokesman in the House of Commons; memoranda by Salisbury's private secretaries on specific matters, including a minute by Curzon on plans for a Paris exhibition 1900; correspondence with under-secretaries including three letters from Curzon 1897–98 on Crete, Mesopotamia, and trade with Persia; correspondence with diplomats, foreign rulers, and others (arranged alphabetically) and correspondence arranged by country, including extensive material 1895–1900 for Egypt, France, and Turkey.

Correspondence with prominent politicians (Class E): includes letters (143) 1884–1902 from Curzon as under-secretary for India (9), for foreign affairs (86), as viceroy (15), etc.

Marquess of Salisbury. Inquiries to the Librarian and Archivist, Hatfield House, Hertfordshire AL9 5NF. NRA 9226 (Foreign Office correspondence only).

Chamberlain, Sir (Joseph) Austen (1863–1937). Financial secretary to the Treasury 1900–2; postmaster-general 1902–3; chancellor of the exchequer 1903–5, 1919–21; secretary for India 1915–17; foreign secretary 1924–29.

45. Extensive correspondence with Curzon, especially 1905–25, including letters relating to many aspects of Chamberlain's government responsibilities during this period and much on India 1915–20.

Birmingham University Library, West Midlands. NRA 12604.

Charteris, Mary Constance, Countess of Wemyss (1861–1937).

46. Correspondence and papers including letters from her brother George Wyndham, her husband, and other members of her family 1869–1937, fellow "Souls" such as Balfour, Curzon (1 bundle 1890–1914 including records of his farewell dinner 1898), Wilfred Scawen Blunt, Brodrick, and members of the Asquith family 1877–1937; diaries, photograph albums, commonplace books, etc., 1878–1937; letter from her to J.W. Mackail 1922 relating to Curzon's return from India in 1905.

Earl of Wemyss. Enquiries to Lord Neidpath, Stanway, Cheltenham, Gloucestershire. NRA 9751.

Churchill, Lord Randolph Henry Spencer (1849–1894). Secretary for India 1885–86; chancellor of the exchequer 1886.

47. Correspondence with Curzon 1887–94 (36 items).

Churchill Archives Centre, Churchill College, Cambridge (RCHL). NRA 13273.

Churchill, Sir Winston Leonard Spencer (1874–1965). Under-secretary for the colonies 1905–8; president of the Board of Trade 1908–10; home secretary 1910–11; 1st. lord of the Admiralty 1911–15; chancellor of the Duchy of Lancaster 1915; minister of munitions 1917–19; secretary for war and air 1919–21; colonial secretary 1921–22; chancellor of the exchequer 1924–29.

48. Churchill's papers in the Churchill Archives Centre Cambridge, remain closed to research.

Clarke, Sir Edward George (1841–1931). Conservative M.P. for South-wark, Plymouth, and the City of London 1880–1900, 1906; solicitor-general 1886–92.

49. Correspondence and papers 1880–1906, mainly political and legal and including letters (c.10) 1905–11 relating to literary matters, personal affairs, rights of hereditary peers, and Curzon's possible candidature for the City of London 1905.

Formerly in the possession of his honour Edward Clarke Q.C. (d. 1989), 19 Old Buildings, Lincoln's Inn, London WC2. No more recent information is available. NRA 30373.

Dawson, Geoffrey (1874–1944). Editor of The Times *1912–19, 1923–41.*

50. Special correspondence with Lord Milner and others 1904–23; general correspondence and papers: papers relating to the government's conduct of the war; correspondence with Curzon 1911–18 (15 items) on Sir George Turner, war matters, the Curragh rebellion, etc.; Dawson's notes of conversations with Curzon 1913–15; correspondence 1928 with Lord Stamfordham (private secretary to George V) relating to Baldwin's assumption of the premiership 1923.

Bodleian Library, Oxford University (MSS. Dawson). NRA 25619.

Dilke, Sir Charles Wentworth, 2nd. Baronet (1843–1911). Radical M.P., author.

51. Papers (168 vols.) including correspondence with Curzon 1889–1905 (Add. MS. 43893).

British Library, London (Add. MSS. 43874–967, 49385–455, 49610–12).

Durand, Sir Henry Mortimer (1850–1924). Foreign secretary to the government of India 1884–94; minister to Persia 1894–1900.

52. Correspondence and papers relating to India, Afghanistan, Persia, etc. 1840–1917, including "early" letters from Curzon.

School of Oriental and African Studies, London University (Acc. 257247). NRA 14595.

53. Letter books 1870–1903 and correspondence and papers relating to the Afghan Boundary Commission 1884–1908.

India Office Library and Records, London (MSS. Eur. D729). NRA 27462.

Edward VII, King (1841–1910). See below, under Victoria, Queen.

Elliot-Murray-Kynynmound, Gilbert John, 4th. Earl of Minto (1845–1914). Governor-general of Canada 1898–1904; viceroy of India 1905–10.

54. General correspondence and papers including correspondence with Curzon relating to portraits of Warren Hastings at Calcutta 1898–1913; Indian papers, including bound volumes of printed summaries of Curzon's administration 1899–1905, papers concerning India's foreign relations with Tibet, Afghanistan, and Persia, and to railways, industry, etc.; a record of Kitchener's administration of the Indian army 1902–9; military department proceedings concerning reorganization 1904–5, including a memorandum by Kitchener in reply to an article by John and Richard Strachey, "Playing with fire: Mr. Brodrick and Lord Curzon" (no. 435 below); papers relating to the partition of Bengal; correspondence with the King, including some relating to his appointment, and with Morley, Brodrick, Godley, and others; correspondence with Curzon 1905 relating to the handing over of office.

National Library of Scotland, Edinburgh (MSS. 12365–803 passim). NRA 10476.

Emmott, Alfred, Baron Emmott (1858–1926). First commissioner of works 1914–15; director of the War Trade Department 1915–19; chairman of the Foreign Office Committee to collect information on Russia 1920–21.

55. Diaries, correspondence and memoranda, press cuttings, and miscellaneous papers 1894–1926, including correspondence with Curzon (c.20 items) 1912–22 mainly relating to the Foreign Office Russia committee 1920–21.

Nuffield College Library, Oxford. NRA 17309.

Forrest, Sir George William David Starck (1845–1926). Historian of India, biographer of Lord Clive and Lord Roberts.

56. Letters (24) from Curzon and others 1892–1916 mainly relating to Indian history.

Bodleian Library, Oxford University (MSS. Eng. lett. c.213 ff. 180–245; d.275 ff. 48–85; e.116 ff. 142–63; c.291 ff. 238–342; e.133 ff. 137–75).

Foster, Sir William (1863–1951). Historian of India, registrar, and superintendent of records at the India Office 1907–27.

57. Letters (20) from Curzon 1906–25.

India Office Library and Records (MSS. Eur. E242). NRA 27488.

Fryer, Sir Frederick William Richards (1845–1922). Lieutenant-governor of Burma 1897–1903.

58. Diaries 1860–1927, including volumes for his lieutenant-governorship in Burma, 1886–1903; private correspondence with Curzon 1899 relating to Burmese administration.

India Office Library and Records, London (MSS. Eur. E355). NRA 27503.

George V, King (1865–1936). See below, Victoria, Queen.

Gladstone, William Ewart (1809–1898). Statesman.

59. Correspondence and papers, including letters (10) from Curzon 1878–97 (Add. MSS. 44456–526 passim).
British Library, London (Add. MSS. 44086–835).

Godley, Sir Arthur, 1st. Baron Kilbracken (1847–1932). Permanent under-secretary for India 1883–1909.

60. Letterbooks 1883–1909 (2 vols.); letters to him from secretaries for India including Lord George Hamilton 1895–1903 and St. John Brodrick 1903–5, from viceroys including Curzon 1898–1904 and Lord Minto 1905–9, from Lord Ampthill (governor of Madras 1903–6 and acting viceroy 1904) and other Indian administrators, mainly before 1898 but including correspondence with Curzon relating to his relations with the Cabinet 1904–5, and material on the Indian Army 1905.
India Office Library and Records, London (MSS. Eur. F102). NRA 27523.

Gosse, Sir Edmund William (1847–1928). Librarian, critic, and man of letters.

61. Letters (61) from Curzon 1893–1921, mainly on literary and social matters, including Curzon's family history, translations of verse by Verhaeren and other writers, and a knighthood for Gosse.
The Brotherton Collection, Leeds University Library, West Yorkshire. See *The Gosse correspondence in the Brotherton Collection*, Leeds, 1950.

Grenfell, Ethel Anne Priscilla, Baroness Desborough (1867–1952).

62. Letters (21) from Curzon 1889–1920 and n.d. and from other "Souls," including Balfour, George Wyndham, and Lord and Lady Elcho.
Hertfordshire Record Office, Hertford (D/ERV). NRA 26768.

Hamilton, Lord George Francis (1845–1927). Secretary for India 1895–1903.

63. Indian correspondence and papers, including private correspondence with Curzon 1899–1903, Lord Elgin 1897–98, and the King 1901–3; private telegrams (including drafts and copies) to and from Curzon 1899–1903; papers arranged by subject, including Persia and Curzon's tour of the Gulf, the North-West Frontier, Afghanistan, China, Tibet, Edward VII's accession and the coronation Durbar, Curzon's relations with the secretary of state's council in London, Curzon's education policies and disciplinary measures in the Indian Army.
India Office Library and Records, London (MSS. Eur. F123). NRA 10867.

64.   Private correspondence with Curzon 1899–1903.
India Office Library and Records, London (MSS. Eur. D508–10, C125–6).
NRA 10867.

Hardinge, Charles, 1st. Baron Hardinge of Penshurst (1858–1944).
Viceroy of India 1910–16; ambassador to France 1920–22; permanent
under-secretary for foreign affairs 1906–10, 1916–20.

65.   Correspondence and papers as foreign under-secretary and ambassador to
France, including letters (c. 15) from Curzon c.1903–22; letters (c.7) to him as
viceroy from Curzon 1910–16.
Cambridge University Library. See *Handlist of the Hardinge papers*, 1968.

66.   Diplomatic and Indian correspondence and papers c.1906–24, including
letters from Curzon praising his achievements in Paris, congratulating him on
his appointment as viceroy, etc.
Kent Archives Office, Maidstone, Kent (U927, 2348). NRA 8909.

Hicks-Beach, Sir Michael Edward, 1st. Earl St. Aldwyn (1837–1916).
Chancellor of the exchequer 1885–86, 1895–1902; chief secretary for
Ireland 1886–87; president of the Board of Trade 1888–92.

67.   Correspondence and papers including letters from Curzon and others to
him and his wife 1883–1915.
Gloucestershire Record Office, Gloucester (D2455). NRA 3526.

Herbert, Sir Michael Henry (1857–1903). Secretary of embassy in Tur-
key, Italy, and France 1894–1902; ambassador to the United States of
America 1902–3.

68.   Diplomatic correspondence 1882–1903, including letters from Curzon, Salisbury, other politicians, diplomats, and members of the royal household.
Wiltshire Record Office, Trowbridge (WRO 2057). NRA 22080.

Herbert, Sidney, 14th. Earl of Pembroke (1853–1913). Lord steward
of the household 1895–1905.

69.   Correspondence with Salisbury, George Wyndham, Curzon, and other
politicians 1890–1912.
Wiltshire Record Office, Trowbridge (WRO 2057). NRA 22080.

Houtum-Schindler, Sir Albert (d.1916). Engineer and authority on
Persia.

70.   Letters from Curzon c.1889–1912 relating to Curzon's book, *Persia and*
the Persian Question, to Persian relations with Britain and Russia, the Persian
Bank Mining Rights Corporation, and political figures in Britain and Russia;

draft memorandum by Houtum-Schindler concerning the opening of the Karun River to commerce, Russo-Persian boundary questions, etc.
   William R. Perkins Library, Duke University, Durham, N. Carolina.

   Howard, Esmé William, 1st. Baron Howard of Penrith (1863–1939). Member of the British delegation to the Paris Peace Conference 1919; ambassador to Spain 1919–24; to the United States of America 1924–30.

71.   Diaries 1891–1927; diplomatic correspondence and papers, including material on the peace conference, setting up of the League of Nations, Spanish and American affairs; copies of official dispatches between him and the Foreign Office 1889–1930; private correspondence with Curzon 1898–1924, Lord Hardinge 1906–10, 1916–20, and others 1902–39.
   Cumbria Record Office, Carlisle (DHW 1–6). NRA 23774.

   Jowett, Benjamin (1817–93). Master of Balliol College, Oxford.

72.   Correspondence and papers, including correspondence with Curzon.
   Balliol College Archives, Oxford University.

   Kerr, Philip Henry, 11th. Marquess of Lothian (1882–1940). Private secretary to David Lloyd George 1916–21, newspaper editor.

73.   Papers as private secretary to Lloyd George 1917–21, including correspondence with Curzon, Balfour, and others on Middle Eastern affairs 1917–20; correspondence with Sir Eric Drummond (private secretary to the foreign secretary) on a wide range of foreign policy matters 1918–20, including extensive material on the Paris Peace Conference; memoranda, correspondence, and other papers relating to Italian claims in the Adriatic 1919–20, including notes and letters from Curzon and Italian politicians; letters to Kerr as editor of the *Daily Chronicle* 1921–22, including some from Curzon complaining about articles on the Foreign Office February 1921; general correspondence 1918–21, including letters from Curzon on British representation at the peace conference and negotiations with Turkey 1919–20, and correspondence with many British and foreign statesmen on reparations, the peace conference, etc.
   Scottish Record Office, Edinburgh (GD 40). NRA 10737.

   Keyes, Brigadier-General Sir Terence Humphrey (1877–1939). On famine duty in Central Provinces 1900; vice-consul in Seistan and Kain 1903; consul in Turbat-i-Haidari 1906; served in Baluchistan 1908, 1921–28; political agent in the Persian Gulf 1914; attached to the Russian army in Romania 1917; on special duty in Russia 1917–20.

74.   Military reports, Cabinet papers, memoranda, and copies of correspondence with Curzon and others relating to the British military mission in south Russia 1917–20; copies of telegrams between the British mission and the Foreign

Office 1920; memoranda, correspondence, and other papers relating to Russia 1919–20, including Jewish pógroms, the economy, etc.

India Office Library and Records, London (MSS. Eur. E131). NRA 27529.

Kitchener, Horatio Herbert, 1st. Earl Kitchener of Khartoum and Broome (1850–1916). Commander-in-chief in India 1902–9.

75. Indian papers, including correspondence with St. John Brodrick, Curzon (16 items), Lord Roberts, Lord Ampthill, Lord George Hamilton, Lord Minto, and others 1900–12; letters and papers relating to "dual control" 1903–6; Kitchener's "Note on the military policy of India" (1905); press cuttings 1900–11; War Cabinet papers, including correspondence with Curzon, Lloyd George, Lord Selborne, Lord Fisher, and other members of the Cabinet 1914–16; Sir George Arthur's papers and letters for his biography of Kitchener 1916–38.

Public Record Office, Kew, Surrey (PRO 30/57). NRA 7283.

Law, Andrew Bonar (1858–1923). Leader of the Conservative Party from 1911; colonial secretary 1915–16; chancellor of the exchequer 1916–18; lord privy seal 1918–21; prime minister 1922–23.

76. Political correspondence and papers, including letters (c.112) from Curzon to Law as leader of the Conservative Party 1911–15 relating to women's suffrage, Ireland, compulsory military service, etc.; as colonial secretary 1915–16 relating to deficiencies of munitions, Air Board matters, and national service; as chancellor of the exchequer 1916–18 relating to the composition of the coalition government, Ireland, the military service bill, etc.; as lord privy seal and prime minister 1918–23 mainly relating to foreign affairs (Persia, Turkey, Lausanne, etc.).

House of Lords Record Office, London. NRA 19286.

Lawrence, Sir Walter Roper, 1st. Baronet (1857–1940). Private secretary to Curzon 1898–1903.

77. Diaries 1901–2; Indian correspondence and papers, including letters from Curzon 1895–1924 and Lord Roberts 1895–1914, letters of congratulation on his appointment as Curzon's private secretary 1898, correspondence with Curzon and the viceroy's council 1901–5, copies and drafts of speeches, etc. relating to India, including biographical and autobiographical notes; press cuttings 1885–1940.

India Office Library and Records, London (MSS. Eur. F143). NRA 27535.

Lloyd George, David, 1st Earl Lloyd-George of Dwyfor (1863–1945). Minister of munitions 1915–16; secretary for war 1916; prime minister 1916–22.

78. Correspondence and papers as minister for munitions, including correspondence with Curzon on national service, Air Board matters, munitions; as prime minister, including correspondence (270 letters) with Curzon on the Air Board, appointments, parliamentary business, and (from 1918) foreign affairs: the Paris Peace Conference, possible trial of the Kaiser, Egypt, Persia, Turkey, Anglo-Russian relations, Palestine and the Mesopotamian mandates, reparations and the occupation of the Ruhr, etc; correspondence on foreign affairs with members of the Cabinet, British and foreign politicians and others 1916–22; further papers on foreign policy arranged by subject, including the Near and Middle East, France, Germany, the United States, etc.; correspondence and papers of Lloyd George's secretariat (his "garden suburb"), including memoranda of meetings involving Curzon, draft conventions, copies of letters and other papers by Curzon; papers 1922–45, mainly after 1925 and including special correspondence with Balfour, Chamberlain, and others and general correspondence on foreign affairs; press cuttings relating to his career, including one file concerning Curzon 1922–24.

House of Lords Record Office, London. NRA 15700.

Lyttelton, Alfred (1857–1913). Colonial secretary 1903–5.

79. Political correspondence and papers, including letters from Balfour, Chamberlain, and Curzon (20 items) 1886–98 and n.d.; letters (12) from Curzon to his wife Edith Lyttelton 1889–1913 and n.d.

Churchill Archive Centre, Churchill College, Cambridge. NRA 19700.

Macmillan and Company, publishers.

80. Correspondence with Curzon 1895–1915 and n.d.

British Library, London (Add. MS. 55245).

Malcolm, Sir Ian Zachary (1868–1944). Private secretary to Lord Salisbury 1895–98 and to A. J. Balfour 1916–19 as foreign secretaries; Curzon's literary executor.

81. Diaries 1895–1900, 1910, and 1918–19, the last relating to the Paris Peace Conference; miscellaneous correspondence and papers 1887–1940, including a printed magazine article "Lord Curzon, viceroy and friend of India, 1903."

R.N.L. Malcolm Esq. Enquiries about access to NRA (Scotland), Scottish Record Office, West Register House, Charlotte Square, Edinburgh. NRA 15645.

Marker, Colonel Raymond John (1867–1914). A.D.C. to Curzon as viceroy 1899–1900, to Lord Kitchener in South Africa and India 1901–6.

82. Papers relating to Kitchener's accounts c.1900–2; correspondence with General Hubert Hamilton and others on Indian army administration c.1902–6; copies of telegrams between Curzon and Kitchener 1905 and of decyphered

telegrams from Kitchener to Marker 1910 relating to the dispute with Curzon, printed memorandum by Kitchener on army reform 1905, etc.
National Army Museum, London.

Milner, Alfred, Viscount Milner (1854–1925). High commissioner for South Africa 1897–1905; member of the War Cabinet 1916; secretary for war 1918; colonial secretary 1918–21.

83.   Extensive political correspondence and papers, including letters (c.85) from Curzon relating to South Africa, Egypt, War Office matters, colonial and foreign affairs 1898–1921.
Bodleian Library, Oxford University (MSS. Milner Dep. 1–684, MSS. Eng. hist. c.686–709, d.362, e.305–7). NRA 14300.

Morley, John, Viscount Morley of Blackburn (1838–1923). Secretary for India 1905–10, 1911; lord president of the council 1910–14.

84.   Correspondence and papers as secretary for India 1890–1915, mainly 1905–11, including private telegrams (25) between St. John Brodrick (his predecessor) and Curzon 1903–5; letters, telegrams and minutes from Arthur Godley to Morley relating to the "dual control" controversy involving Curzon, Kitchener, and the home government 1904–6; correspondence, and related papers, with Curzon on records of his viceroyalty 1906–10, Tibet and the Victoria Memorial 1906–7, the Clive Memorial 1907–8, frontier reports, the ascent of Mount Everest, proposals for an honor for Curzon 1906–9, and the Imperial Institute.
India Office Library and Records, London (MSS. Eur. D573). NRA 10408.

85.   Printed and typescript copies of memoranda, reports, and dispatches on Indian military administration 1852–1909, mainly relating to "dual control" and bearing Morley's annotations.
India Office Library and Records, London (MSS. Eur. D717).

Orange, Sir Hugh William (1866–1956). First director-general of education in India.

86.   Notes on Curzon, Kitchener, Sir Walter Lawrence, and others, and comments on the Universities Commission of 1902 and Curzon's policy reforms; letters from India to his parents referring to Curzon's standing in Indian public opinion, his relations with Kitchener, speculation over his successor, etc. 1903–5.
Cambridge South Asian Archive, Cambridge University.

Palmer, William Waldegrave, 2nd. Earl of Selborne (1859–1942). Under-secretary for the colonies 1895–1900; first lord of the Admiralty 1900–5; high commissioner for South Africa 1905–10; president of the Board of Agriculture 1915–16.

87.   Special correspondences with Balfour, Salisbury, Chamberlain, Brodrick, and others 1882–1941, including Curzon (206 leaves) 1882–1924; subject files

of papers and further correspondence with Curzon 1881–1905 relating to the Colonial Office, Admiralty, War Cabinet, etc.
Bodleian Library, Oxford University (MSS. Selborne 1–222). NRA 17810.

Rendel, Stuart, 1st. Baron Rendel (1834–1913). President of University College, Wales from 1895, M.P.

88.   Personal and social correspondence with Curzon and others 1878–1912.
National Library of Wales, Aberystwyth, Dyfed.

Richards, Sir Henry Erle (1861–1922). Legal member of the viceroy's council 1904–9.

89.   Indian correspondence and papers including letters (9) from Curzon relating to Richards's appointment, Indian army supply and transport matters, Curzon's resignation, etc. 1904–5; travel journals in India, notebooks, albums of press cuttings 1904–5.
India Office Library and Records, London (MSS. Eur. F 122). NRA 10868.

Roberts, Frederick Sleigh, 1st. Earl Roberts of Kandahar (1832–1914). Commander-in-chief in India 1885–93; supreme commander in South Africa 1899–1900; commander-in-chief 1900–5.

90.   Correspondence and papers, including correspondence with Brodrick 1885–1913, Curzon 1894–1914, Churchill 1900–14, Kitchener 1898–1914, Milner 1898–1922, other soldiers, colonial administrators, and statesmen; papers relating to India, the "dual system" dispute between Curzon and Kitchener, the national service movement in Britain, etc.
National Army Museum, London (Acc 7101–23). NRA 18656.

Royal Geographical Society.

91.   Correspondence (c.400 items) with the Society relating to his travels, his presidency, etc. 1890–1917; observations of temperatures and altitudes in the Pamirs 1894; press cuttings of articles written for *The Times* 1894; an account of Sir Francis Younghusband's expedition to Chitral ("Across the Indian frontier") 1895, with press cuttings.
Royal Geographical Society Library, London.

Rumbold, Sir Horace George Montagu, 9th. Baronet (1869–1941). Minister to Switzerland 1916–19, to Poland 1919–20; ambassador to Turkey 1920–24; deputy to Curzon at the Lausanne Conference 1922–23.

92.   Diplomatic correspondence and papers 1876–1941, including correspondence with Curzon 1919–24 mainly relating to his embassy to Turkey and to the Lausanne Conference 1920–23 (c.30 items).
Bodleian Library, Oxford University (MS. Rumbold dep.). NRA 22147.

Russell, Arthur Oliver Villiers, 2nd. Baron Ampthill (1869–1935). Governor of Madras 1900–6; acting viceroy 1904.

93.   Indian papers including correspondence as governor of Madras and acting viceroy during Curzon's absence with secretaries of state, Indian princes, and with Curzon in England and in India relating to the Durbar of 1903, Afghanistan and foreign affairs, Madras budgetary matters, etc.

India Office Library and Records, London (MSS. Eur. E 233). NRA 27486.

Samuel, Herbert Louis, 1st. Viscount Samuel (1870–1963). Postmaster-general and chancellor of the Duchy of Lancaster 1915–16; home secretary 1916; chairman of the select committee on national expenditure 1917–18; special commissioner to Belgium 1919; high commissioner for Palestine 1920–25.

94.   General political papers 1888–1962, including letters (57) from Asquith, Grey, Lloyd George, Curzon, and others; subject correspondence 1890–1962, including letters (5) from Curzon on Samuel's appointment as home secretary 1916 and to his Belgian mission 1919.

House of Lords Record Office, London. NRA 11187.

95.   Correspondence and papers (20 volumes) as high commissioner for Palestine 1920–25.

State Archives of Israel, Jerusalem. Copies are held by the House of Lords Record Office, London.

Scott, (Edith Agnes) Kathleen (1878–1947). Sculptor and widow of Robert Falcon Scott, Antarctic explorer.

96.   Letters (11) from Curzon relating to Scott's expedition, his death, and the proposed publication of his diaries in *Strand Magazine* 1912–13, and letters (2) to Scott 1912–13 which arrived in the Antarctic after his death and were returned to Curzon.

Scott Polar Research Institute, Cambridge University.

Spring Rice, Sir Cecil Arthur (1858–1918). Ambassador to the U.S.A. 1913–18.

97.   Papers including correspondence with Curzon (c.70 pp.) 1884–1904 and with Mary Curzon (78 pp.) 1888–1904.

Churchill College Archives, Cambridge University. NRA 5574.

Stanley, Edward George Villiers, 17th. Earl of Derby (1865–1948). Secretary for war 1916–18, 1922–24, ambassador to France 1918–20.

98.   War Office papers 1916–18, including correspondence with Lloyd George, papers concerning the Air Board, etc.; papers as ambassador to France 1918–20, including correspondence with Balfour as foreign secretary 1916–19, R.H.

Campbell (Curzon's private secretary at the Foreign Office), Sir Eyre Crowe, and Lord Hardinge 1916–20, Curzon 1920 and with other statesmen and diplomats; as secretary for war 1922–24, including correspondence with Balfour and Curzon; special correspondence with particular statesmen, including Curzon 1912, 1920–24 (2 folders), Balfour, Churchill, and others; correspondence with British diplomats in France while out of office 1922–28, 1928–34, etc.; miscellaneous papers, including material relating to reform of the House of Lords 1911–12.

Liverpool Record Office, Merseyside (920 DER 17). NRA 20761.

Strachey, John St. Loe (1860–1927). Editor and proprietor of The Spectator *1898–1925.*

99.   Papers, including correspondence (56 items) 1905–24 with Curzon relating to his resignation as viceroy, reform of Oxford University, free trade, the constitutional crisis of 1911–12, and his contributions to *The Spectator*; correspondence with Balfour, Law, Milner, Spring Rice, Lord Stamfordham, and others c.1890–1927.

House of Lords Record Office, London. NRA 19285.

Tower, Sir Reginald (1860–1939). Minister to Siam 1901–3, the Argentine 1910–19, Paraguay 1911–19; high commissioner of the League of Nations at Danzig 1919–20.

100.   Papers, including press cuttings, etc. 1895–1921, and a volume entitled "Reports etc." 1892–1901 comprising Command Papers to which he had contributed and dispatches addressed to him by Rosebery, Curzon, Salisbury, and others.

Foreign and Commonwealth Office Library, London.

Victoria, Queen (1819–1901).

101.   Letters from Curzon to Victoria (40), Edward VII (50), George V (20), together with a number of letters to Lord Stamfordham and other private secretaries c.1898–1925.

Royal Archives, Windsor Castle, Berkshire. Applications for admission should be addressed to the Librarian. Access is normally restricted to post-doctoral research leading to publication.

Vincent, Sir Edgar, 1st. Viscount d'Abernon (1857–1941). Financier and ambassador to Germany 1920–26.

102.   Diplomatic papers, including correspondence with Curzon 1902–20 (1 volume), relating to his embassy to Germany 1920–24 (4 volumes), to British and German casualty figures during the war 1921–26, and to the national galleries 1907–31 (2 volumes).

British Library, London (Add. MSS. 48923–5B, 48927, 48930).

White, Sir Herbert Thirkell (1855–1931). Chief judge of the chief court of lower Burma 1902–5; lieutenant-governor of Burma 1905–10.

103.   Correspondence and papers mainly relating to the administration of Burma, including correspondence with Curzon 1901–5.
India Office Library and Records, London (MSS. Eur. E 254). NRA 27489.

Wilson, Field Marshal Sir Henry Hughes, 1st. Baronet (1864–1922). Chief of the Imperial General Staff 1918–22.

104.   Papers including correspondence (62 items) as chief of staff with Curzon 1918–20 relating to French activity in Armenia, the evacuation of Batum, events in Palestine, withdrawals from Persia, Greek operations in Asia Minor, Anglo-Russian relations, etc.; diaries 1893–1922.
Imperial War Museum, London (DS/MISC/80). NRA 28567.

Wyndham, George (1863–1913). Under-secretary for war 1898–1900; chief secretary for Ireland 1900–5.

105.   Personal correspondence of Curzon with Wyndham and his wife, Sibell, formerly Lady Grosvenor from c.1880.
Duke of Westminster, Eaton Estate Office, Eccleston, Cheshire CH4 9ET.

Younghusband, Sir Francis Edward (1863–1942). Explorer and Indian political officer; headed British expedition to Tibet 1903–4.

106.   Correspondence and papers c.1885–1903 relating to relations with tribes on the North-West Frontier, famine in India, religious instruction for Hindus, including a draft letter to Curzon 1902; to his Tibetan mission 1903–4, including correspondence with Curzon 1903–5 and Lord Ampthill 1904, papers relating to the treaty he negotiated with Tibet and notes, etc. concerning censures by the India Office for exceeding his instructions; papers of Lady Younghusband relating to the Tibetan mission 1903–c.1930, including correspondence with Lord Ronaldshay for his *Life* of Curzon 1928–29; family correspondence and papers, including letters to his wife from Tibet 1903–4; general correspondence, including letters from Lord Roberts 1890–1905, Curzon 1893–c.1924, Lord Birdwood 1914–29, and others; miscellaneous correspondence including drafts, copies, etc. of letters to Curzon on religious matters ?1914; diaries, notebooks, etc., including his impressions in his 1894 diary of Curzon during the latter's visit to Chitral, and "notes for interview with Ld. Curzon. Port Said. Nov. 24/04"; MS. and published writings, including "Lord Curzon's religion" n.d.; press cuttings relating to the Tibetan mission, including letters from him to the press on this subject and on Curzon's resignation.
India Office Library and Records, London (MSS. Eur. F. 197). NRA 29781.

C. OFFICIAL PAPERS

1. Foreign Office

The official records of the Foreign Office, which are held by the Public Record Office, are more fully described in *The records of the Foreign Office* (no. 17 above). The following groups of records within the Foreign Office (FO) class include material relating to Curzon's periods of office as under-secretary 1895–98 and foreign secretary 1919–24.

107.   Registers of general diplomatic, commercial, consular, and treaty correspondence 1817–1920 (FO 566).

108.   Numerical (central) registers of general correspondence 1906–20 (FO 662).

109.   Indexes to general correspondence 1891–1905 (FO 804). There is also a card index, with annual indexes of subjects, persons, and places, 1906–20.

110.   Annual printed indexes of subjects, persons, and places, including indexes to "green [i.e., secret] papers" (FO 409).

111.   General correspondence before 1906 arranged by country, continent, or region, e.g., Belgium 1830–1905 (FO 10), Africa 1825–1905 (FO 2), and Asia, Central 1899–1905 (FO 106). The series includes dispatches to and from the Foreign Office and British diplomats abroad, and communications between the Foreign Office and foreign representatives in Britain (FO 1–82).

112.   General correspondence since 1906 arranged according to Foreign Office department. The following groups relate to Curzon's period as foreign secretary: commercial 1906–20 (FO 368), consular 1906–41 (FO 369), contraband 1915–20 (FO 382), library 1906–41 (FO 370), news 1916–38 (FO 395), political, including the political intelligence department 1918–20, 1906–41 (FO 371), prisoners of war 1915–19 (FO 383), and treaty 1906–41 (FO 372).

113.   Great War records 1914–18, including papers relating to the Arab Bureau 1911–20 (FO 882), foreign trade department 1916–19, Jedda Agency 1913–25, temporary departments such as the ministry of blockade 1915–19 (FO 902), restriction of enemy supplies department 1916–19 (FO 845).

114.   Chief clerk's department archives 1719–1940 (FO 366).

115.   Private office "individual" files 1904–42 comprising selected correspondence relating to senior diplomats and Foreign Office officials.

116.   Treaty papers, including protocols 1778–1962 (FO 93) and ratifications 1782–1966 (FO 94), both groups arranged by country.

117.   Passport office papers, including correspondence 1815–1905 (FO 612), registers of correspondence 1868–1905 (FO 613), correspondence with British embassies, etc., 1886, 1897–1900 (FO 614), registers of passports 1795–1898 (FO 610–11), representative case papers 1920–54 (FO 737).

118.   Cabinet papers (FO 899).

119.   Confidential print: copies of important telegrams, dispatches, etc., circulated to government departments, the monarch, and others, and periodically printed 19th–20th century.

120.   Archives of commissions, including some filed among the Cabinet Office (Cab) and War Office (WO) records: Allied High Commission at Archangel correspondence 1918–19 (FO 175), Klagenfurt (Austria) Plebiscite Commission 1920 (FO 895), Inter-Allied Rhineland High Commission 1920–30 (FO 894), Inter-Allied Armistice Commission 1918–20 (WO 144), Mixed Arbitral Tribunals 1921–31 (FO 324–8, 897), Paris Exhibition of 1900 (FO 311), Reparation Commission 1919–31, International (Schleswig) Plebiscite Commission 1919–21, Inter-Allied (Upper Silesia) Administration and Plebiscite Commission 1920–22, Allied High Commission at Vladivostok 1918–21, Allied (War) Conferences 1915–19 (Cab 25), Conference at Lausanne 1922–23 (FO 839), international conferences 1916–39 including the Paris Peace Conference 1919–20 and the London Reparations Conference 1924 (Cab 29), Washington Disarmament Conference 1921–22 (Cab 30), Conference at Genoa 1922 (Cab 31), and the Paris Peace Conference 1919–20 (FO 373–4, 608).

2. India Office

The following classes of official India Office and government of India records relate to Curzon's periods as under-secretary 1891–92 and as viceroy 1898–1905. A summary of each class is given below, followed by its reference in brackets. They are held by the India Office Library and Records in London. Fuller details of the papers and of the department or body producing them are provided in Martin Moir, *A general guide to the India Office records* (no. 12 above).

121.   Minutes and memoranda of the Council of India which exercised advisory and controlling powers over the secretary of state in London 1854–1947 (Class C).

122.   India Office economic department records 1786–1950, comprising papers of the principal departments concerned with revenue, social, and economic questions, with related correspondence and collections files. For Curzon's period subjects include Indian agriculture, archaeology, emigration, famine, and land revenue (Class L/E).

123.   India Office financial department records c. 1800–1948, covering for the period after 1858 subjects such as currency and exchange, financial powers of the government of India, income tax, civil and military expenditure, and finance for railways, irrigation, and public works. The records include internal India Office correspondence, correspondence with India, departmental files and collections, and papers of commissions and committees of enquiry (Class L/F).

124. Legal adviser's records c. 1550–c.1950, including parliamentary committee papers and drafts of bills 1832–1935, papers relating to cases involving the government of India in court and settled out of court 1704–1947, contracts for railways and other general works 1815–1946, and royal warrants, copies, and drafts appointing viceroys, etc. 1830–1943 (Class L/L).

125. India Office military department records 1707–1957, including correspondence with India 1803–1937, compilations and miscellaneous papers on major campaigns and expeditions, etc. 1754–1944, military collections on all aspects of military policy and administration c.1850–1950, and printed library reference material on the Indian frontier region and areas where the government of India had military interests such as Japan, the Middle East, and Persia (Class L/MIL).

126. Parliamentary branch records c. 1772–1952, including collections of parliamentary papers on subjects of interest to the India Office c. 1772–1943 (Class L/PARL).

127. Private office papers c.1858–1948, comprising papers kept by the private secretaries of successive secretaries for India and including material on economic and financial matters, Indian defense, and foreign policy (Class L/PO).

128. India Office public works department records 1839–1931, including correspondence with India, departmental papers, and compilations relating to irrigation, public buildings, railways, municipal engineering, etc. (Class L/PWD).

129. India Office public and judicial department records 1795–1950, including correspondence with India, departmental papers, and compilations relating to the Indian civil service, constitutional reforms, education, Indian emigration, political movements, etc. (Class L/P&J).

130. India Office political and secret department records 1756–c.1950, including correspondence, departmental papers, memoranda, miscellaneous records, and printed library reference material relating to such subjects as French activity in south Asia, Indian relations with Persia, Tibet, and Afghanistan, frontier affairs, relations with princely states in India, political movements, and state functions (Class L/P&S).

131. India Office record department papers 1859–1959, including correspondence, departmental files, and compilations relating to the Victoria Memorial Hall, etc. and weekly reports on the Indian press 1868–1939 (Class L/R).

132. Proceedings and consultations of the viceroy and government of India 1834–1945, including papers relating to foreign affairs, education, municipalities, police, military matters, public works and railways, revenue and agriculture, and archaeology; proceedings of the provincial and presidential governments of Bengal, Bombay, Madras, Punjab, etc. 1702–1945 (Class P).

133.   Commission, committee, and conference records c. 1895–1947, including papers of the Royal Commission on the administration of the expenditure of India (the Welby Commission) 1895–1900 (Class Q).

134.   Crown representative's political department records 1880–1947, comprising papers relating to the special authority of the viceroy over Indian princely states and including correspondence with British Residents, rulers of states, and the India Office in London (Class R/1).

135.   Crown representative's residency records c. 1789–1947, comprising papers relating to the internal affairs of Indian states, including Hyderabad, Kashmir, and Mysore (Class R/2).

136.   Other records of the central and provincial governments c.1899–1944, including viceregal private office papers relating to honors 1899–1947 (Class R/3).

137.   Persian Gulf agency records 1763–1951, including correspondence, subject files, etc. of the British agencies at Bushire, Bahrain, Kuwait, and Muscat (Class R/15).

138.   Records of the British administration of Aden 1837–1967 (Class R/20).

139.   Linguistic survey of India records c.1900–c.1930 (Class S).

140.   Official publications c.1760–1957, including Acts, parliamentary orders, etc. relating to India, parliamentary journals, debates and papers, serials published by the India Office and government of India, gazettes, statistical serials, census reports, archaeological serials, departmental annual reports, monographs on India, etc. (Class V).

141.   Registers and indexes to particular series of India Office and government of India records (Class Z).

3. Cabinet Office

The following groups of Cabinet Office records (all in the Public Record Office) include material relating to Curzon's viceroyalty or cover the period of his membership in the Cabinet.

142.   Miscellaneous records 1866–1922, including papers relating to the dispute between Curzon and Kitchener over Indian military administration 1905 (Cab 1/6/14).

143. Photographic copies of memoranda circulated to the Cabinet before 1916. See *List of Cabinet Office papers 1880–1914* and *List of Cabinet papers 1915 and 1916* (nos. 13–14 above) (Cab 37).

144. Photographic copies of letters from prime ministers to the sovereign 1868–1916 reporting Cabinet proceedings, including letters on Curzon as viceroy 1905, Afghanistan, and the visit to England of the Amir 1906, the Indian Army, Tibet, and other Indian subjects (Cab 41/24/33–30/32).

145. Minutes of Cabinet meetings from 1916 (Cab 23).

146. Memoranda from 1916, comprising papers prepared by government departments or Cabinet Office staff for circulation to members of the Cabinet (Cab 24).

147. Registered files of material on subjects dealt with by the Cabinet from 1916, including material on the Committee of Imperial Defence, the Paris Peace Conference, and other international conferences (Cab 21).

148. Papers of the following Cabinet committees of which Curzon was chairman (all are Cab 27 unless otherwise stated): restriction of imports 1916–17 (Cab 24), Mesopotamia administration 1917 (Cab 21, 27), Gibraltar-Ceuta 1917–19, terms of peace, territorial desiderata 1917 (Cab 21), timber supplies 1917 (Cab 21), soldiers' and sailors' pay 1917–19, Middle-East (which succeeded the Mesopotamia administration committee) 1917–18, allocation of guns 1917, eastern committee (which succeeded the Middle East committee) 1918–19, research 1918–19, peace celebrations 1919, memorial services 1920, House of Lords reform 1920–22, observation of armistice day 1921, situation in Egypt 1921.

149. Minutes, memoranda, correspondence, etc. of the Committee of Imperial Defence (of which Curzon was a member and, from 1924, chairman) relating to home, colonial, and Indian defense 1901–39 (Cab 2–6, 17–18).

150. Minutes, memoranda, etc. of the following sub-committees of the Committee of Imperial Defence: colonial/overseas defense, home (ports) defense, air, coordination of departmental action, imperial communications, air raid precautions, trade questions in time of war, oil board, war legislation, chief of staffs, joint planning, manpower, etc. 1875–1939 (Cab 7–16, 34–6, 46–57 passim).

151. Papers of the following conferences: Allied (War) Conference 1915–19 (Cab 28), British secretariat to the Supreme War Council at Versailles 1917–19 (Cab 25), Peace Conference and other conferences 1916–22 (Cab 29), Washington (Disarmament) Conference 1921–22 (Cab 30), Genoa (International Economic) Conference 1922 (Cab 31), Conferences on Ireland 1921–22 (Cab 43), Imperial Conferences 1917–21 (Cab 32).

4. Other Government Departments

The following groups of official papers are all to be found in the Public Record Office. The appropriate PRO reference is provided in brackets at the end of each entry.

152.   Records of the Air Board and Air Council 1916–52, including minutes of meetings from May 1916 and memoranda, etc. submitted from October 1917 (AIR 6).

153.   Out-letters from the Treasury to other departments and bodies, including the Air Board, 1914–20 (T 114).

154.   Records of the Ministry of Shipping (established 1917 to replace the Shipping Control Committee set up the previous year), including correspondence and papers relating to shipbuilding, conversion of merchant ships, protection against submarines, losses of shipping, tonnage requirements, transport of food and raw materials for industry, etc. 1914–21 (MT 25).

IV. Published Sources

A. CURZON'S WRITINGS

1. Published Books and Articles

155. "An historical parallel." *Oxford Review* 25 February 1885: 135–36.
Article comparing General Charles Gordon (who had recently perished at Khartoum) with Germanicus, nephew of Tiberius.

156. "A purified British senate: the 'status quo.' " *National Review* 11: 61 (March 1888): 115–34.
Proposes reform of the House of Lords to defuse calls for more radical changes or abolition. The House of Commons should represent the middle and lower classes, while the upper house should represent "property, wealth, culture, and administrative ability, which are necessarily the prerogative of the minority." The greatest drawback of the present upper chamber is its hereditary nature which excludes men with experience of imperial government and public service.

157. "A recent journey in Afghanistan." *Journal of the Royal Institution of Great Britain* (1895).
Account of his travels in Afghanistan and meetings with the Amir during 1894–95.

158. "A suggestion on the Elgin Marbles." *Fortnightly Review* (new series) 293 (May 1891): 833–36.
Proposes restoring some elements of the Marbles to the Acropolis site in Athens, but not the melopes, frieze, or torsos which he feared would be destined for an inferior Greek museum.

159. *A viceroy's India. Leaves from Lord Curzon's note-book.* Edited by Peter King. London: Sidgwick and Jackson, 1984. 192.

Selection of Curzon's essays on India from *Leaves from a viceroy's note-book* . . . and *Tales of Travel* (nos. 175 and 200 below) chosen to illustrate Curzon's standing as a travel writer "of the highest order."

160. "A visit to Bokhara the noble." *Fortnightly Review* (new series) 51 (January 1889): 122–43.

Account of his travels in Turkestan in Central Asia and visit to the ancient city of Bokhara during 1888–89.

161. "Sidney Ball" (biographical sketch). (By Curzon, A.J. Carlyle and L.R.F.) *Oxford Magazine* 31 May 1918: 296–97 and 7 June 1918: 306–8.

Memoir of the Oxford graduate renowned for his exploits as a Great War pilot and who was killed in action in 1918.

162. *Bodiam Castle, Sussex. A historical and descriptive survey.* London: Jonathan Cape, 1926. 178.

History of the castle which Curzon purchased and restored; intended to be the first of a "British Mansions Series" researched and written by Curzon.

163. *British government in India: the story of the viceroys and Government House.* London: Cassell and Co., 1925. 2 vols. 527.

History of the government houses occupied by British governors-general and viceroys from William Hedges (1682–84) to 1910. Also included are Curzon's reflections on the individuals concerned.

164. "Conservatism and young Conservatives." *National Review* 8 (January 1887): 577–87.

Enthusiastic exposition of his views on the need for the Tory party to adopt a more radical program and repudiating the charge that Conservatives were a combination of the "prejudices of caste, all the interests of classes, and all the passions of party." Among the institutions to be considered for reform were the House of Lords and the Church.

165. "Conservatives on themselves (part 2): the past and the future of Conservatism." *Fortnightly Review* 43 (old series) 37 (new series) (May 1885): 620–31.

Follow-up to an article (part 1) in the same issue by G.C.T. Bartley on Conservative party organization. He traces the historical development of the Conservative party and identifies a new trend in "Democratic Toryism." The Tories must stand by four fundamental interest groups: State, Church, Empire, and People. The last particularly must not be overlooked by modern Tories lest the masses turn to socialism.

166. *Curzon's Persia.* Edited by Peter King. London: Sidgwick and Jackson, 1986. 192.

Modern edition of Curzon's *Persia and the Persian Question* (no. 189 below).

167. "India between two fires." *Nineteenth Century* 34 (August 1893): 177–86.

In connection with the dual threat to British India posed by the "simultaneous advance" of Russia on the North-West Frontier and by French activity in Siam.

168. "India's memorial to Queen Victoria." *Empire Review* 1 (April 1901): 310–19.

Describes the type of exhibits being sought for the Memorial Hall and the design of the Hall itself.

169. "Kedleston Hall." *Magazine of Art* 21 (May 1897): 20.

Description of the history and architecture of Kedleston Hall.

170. "Leaves from a diary on the Karun River (Part 1)." *Fortnightly Review* 53 (old series) 47 (new series) (April 1890): 479–98.

Account of everyday life on the River Karun, based on Curzon's travels in Persia, which he is concerned to open to external trade.

171. "Leaves from a diary on the Karun River (Part 2)." *Fortnightly Review* 53 (old series) 47 (new series) (May 1890): 694–715.

Concluding part of his Karun River account.

172. "Leaves from a tourist's note-book: Rowsley." *Derby Mercury* 3 August 1881.

First of an early series of published accounts of travels in his native Derbyshire contributed by Curzon to the local press.

173. "Leaves from a tourist's note-book. No. 2: Arbor Law." *Derby Mercury* 7 September 1881.

Part two of a series of travel accounts begun no. 172 above.

174. "Leaves from a tourist's note-book. No. 3: Matlock." *Derby Mercury* 21 September 1881.

Part three of travel series in nos. 172–73 above.

175. *Leaves from a viceroy's note-book, and other papers.* Edited by Ian Malcolm and Francis W. Pember. London: Macmillan, 1926. 424.

Series of essays by Curzon intended as a sequel to *Tales of Travel* (no. 200 below) and published posthumously by his literary executors. They include reminiscences of his viceroyalty (e.g., the gathering of the Mutiny veterans at the great Durbar), and further accounts of his travels in the Pamirs, Levant, north Africa, etc.

176. "Lord Curzon's fifteen reasons against the grant of woman suffrage." *Home Chat* 15 January 1910: 257–58.

Published version for popular consumption of his speech to the Men's League for Opposing Women's Suffrage 18 May 1909.

177. "Map of Persia, with a memorandum and index, prepared for the Royal Geographical Society under the supervision of the Hon. George Curzon, M.P., by W.J.T. Turner F.R.G.S." *Proceedings of the Royal Geographical Society* 14 (February 1892): 69–78.

178. Miscellaneous articles on his visits to French Indo-China: Tonking, Annam, Cochin China, and Cambodia. *Geographical Journal* 2 (August 1893): 97 and (September 1893): 193.
Accounts of the geography, economy, population, etc., of south-east Asia based on his travels in the region during 1892–93.

179. Miscellaneous articles on his visits to the cities of Hue, Annam, Seoul, and Bangkok. *Pall Mall Magazine* 1 (June 1893): 221 and (August 1893): 553; 2 (February 1894): 644.
Popular accounts of his travels in south-east Asia.

180. Miscellaneous series of 17 articles on his travels in Persia. *The Times* November 1889–April 1890.
Series of articles written under contract to *The Times* to help finance his travels describing the geography, culture, etc., of the country as he passed through it.

181. Miscellaneous series of articles on his travels in China, Korea, etc. *The Times* 1892–93.
As in no. 180 above.

182. "Monasteries of the Levant revisited. The Mekeors monastery." *New Review* 5 (December 1891): 515–27.
Account of his visit to the Mekeors monastery with historical, etc., background.

183. "Myth of Er." *Murray's Magazine* September 1887.
Translation of this poem by Curzon in verse, later included in *War Poems* . . . (no. 223 below).

184. *North Meols fisheries. Letter from the Hon. George Curzon M.P.* Southport, 1886. 7.
On the problems of the Ribble fishermen in his Southport constituency with the salmon fishery acts.

185. "Notes from the Nile." *World* 28 March 1883.
An account of current affairs in Egypt based on his travels there.

186. "On England and France in Siam." *North American Review* 157 (September 1893): 268.
Curzon's views on the threat to British influence in the region by French encroachments in Siam.

187. "Our true policy in India: a rejoinder." *National Review* 13 (March 1889): 118–24.

Takes to task earlier articles in the *Fortnightly Review* by "An Indian Officer" (Ian Hamilton) and J.F. Maurice advocating alternative strategies to defend India in the eventuality of a Russian invasion of Afghanistan.

188. *Out of school at Eton.* Privately published, 1877.

An anthology of prose and verse by Curzon and contemporaries at Eton, including Cecil Spring-Rice and J.K. Stephen. Curzon undertook the selection and arrangement of the contributions as his first published work.

189. *Persia and the Persian question.* London: Longmans, Green and Co., 1892. 2 vols. 1290.

Work that helped establish his reputation as an expert on the Middle East. In it he expounds his scheme to protect India against Russia by supporting a series of buffer states between India's northern borders and Russia. The book contains much detail on Persian economic, social, etc., matters and the country's decaying state which necessitated British intervention to bolster it up against possible Russian intervention. Regarded at the time as a masterful study, although more recently doubt has been cast on some of Curzon's statistics.

190. "Poetry, politics and conservatism." *National Review* 6: 34 (December 1885): 502–18.

Holds that poetry should be intellectual and emotional, the expression of truth as well as the utterance of feeling, i.e., content and form both important.

191. "Politics and progress in Siam." *Fortnightly Review* 59 (old series) 53 (new series) (April 1893): 454–67.

Description of the people, religion, economy, government, foreign policy, etc., of Siam, hinting at the threat to British influence in the area of French gunboat and other activity.

192. *Principles and methods of university reform: being a letter addressed to the university of Oxford.* Oxford: Clarendon Press, 1909. 220.

Exposition of his proposals for the reform of the university's constitution.

193. *Problems of the Far East by the Rt. Hon. George Curzon, M.P.: Japan-Korea-China.* London: Longmans, Green and Co., 1896, 2nd edition. 468.

The first edition of the book gave a warning of the growing threat of Japan, and the second edition is able to point to the Japanese defeat of China and the sufferings of Korea during the conflict. Curzon's predictions about the "utter rottenness" of Chinese administration and the certainty of its defeat in war, and of the corrupt though "picturesque imbecility" of Korea were all vindicated. Britain has an important role to play in restructuring eastern Asia. Any chance of Chinese recovery is rejected. The Foreign Office is criticized for not taking Asian affairs sufficiently seriously and he suggests a new department of government to deal solely with Asian affairs to avoid the current division of responsibility between the India Office, the Foreign Office, and the Colonial Office.

194. *Programme of events at the Coronation Durbar, Delhi.* 1903.

Curzon, in typical manner, involved himself in every detail of the planning of the Durbar and compiled the program himself.

195. *Report of the committee on the retention of important works of art in Britain.* 1915. 149.

As a trustee of the National Gallery Curzon initiated moves in 1911 for a committee to inquire into the retention of important pictures in this country. He wrote the eventual report himself and it was presented to parliament in 1915.

196. *Russia in Central Asia in 1889 and the Anglo-Russian question.* London: Longmans, Green and Co., 1889. 500.

Compilation of previously published articles based on his world tour in 1888. He emphasizes his belief in the threat to the security of India posed by Russian policies in the East and the need for Britain to take a firm line against Russian involvement in countries fringing India.

197. "Salvation by torture at Kairwan." *Fortnightly Review* 48 (old series) 42 (new series) (July 1887): 64–76.

Account of the Aissaouia dervishes at the Tanner's Gate, Kairwan, Tunisia.

198. *Memorandum on a proposed Society of "Friends of Art", by Lord Curzon.* Privately printed (?), n.d. 3.

Curzon's aim was to "organize the wealth of the wealthiest art patrons in our midst to mobilize a fund by annual subscription of members" to purchase for the National Gallery masterpieces in private sales or at auction. (Copies included in MSS. Eur. F112/77 among his papers in the India Office Records.

199. "South African politics." *The State* May 1909.

Curzon's views on the current political situation in South Africa. He favors a continuance of the status quo and is against any further extension of the franchise.

200. *Tales of travel.* London: Hodder and Stoughton, 1923. 352. (Reprinted by Century Hutchinson, London, 1988, 344.)

Compilation of travel stories deriving from his world tours, including his meeting with the Amir of Afghanistan, his visit to Napoleon's place of captivity on St. Helena, and his encounter with fanatical dervishes in North Africa. He travelled for two reasons: to see the wonders of the ancient world, and to find out "how far the study of those places and peoples would help . . . [him] form an opinion on the eastern responsibilities and destinies of Great Britain." (p. 3.)

201. *Tattershall Castle Lincolnshire. A historical and descriptive survey by the late Marquis Curzon of Kedleston, K.G. and H. Avray Tipping.* London: Jonathan Cape, 1929. 224.

Conceived by Curzon as the third volume in his series of studies of the houses he owned. His work on Bodiam Castle was published in 1926 (no. 162 above) but he was unable to do anything on Hackwood. He left only a pencil draft of the introduction for the present work, but had collected copious material for the rest of the study on which Tipping was able to base the book. A chapter on Curzon's restoration of the castle is included.

202. "The cloister in Cathay." *Fortnightly Review* 49 (old series) 43 (new series) (June 1888): 752–67.

On the place of Buddhism in Chinese society; mostly incorporated in *Leaves from a viceroy's note-book . . .* and *Problems of the Far East* (nos. 175 and 193 above).

203. "The coalition II." *New Review* 13 (August 1895): 124–28. Signed "Z."

Follow-up to earlier article (no. 222 below) also by "Z" on the abilities of Lord Randolph Churchill and Joseph Chamberlain. Chamberlain should make an excellent colonial secretary but "if he is to succeed he must leave electioneering and wire-pulling to humbler and less encumbered hands." "Z" was identified as Curzon by Chamberlain's biographer J.L. Garvin.

204. "The Conservatism of Tennyson." *Oxford Review* 28 January 1885: 41–42.

Short article for this weekly magazine on the politics of Lord Tennyson whom he had recently visited and whose poetry he greatly admired.

205. "The Conservatism of young Oxford." *National Review* 3: 16 (June 1884): 515–27.

Defends the interest taken in Oxford politics by undergraduates against criticism that they should concentrate on their studies, particularly as the city's politics have become inextricably mixed with the university. He traces the history of the university's involvement in national politics

206. "The destinies of the Far East." *National Review* 21 (May 1893): 315–31.

Based on his travels in countries in the Far East deals with "the part which they are now playing, or are capable of playing, on the international stage." He stresses the importance of British involvement and of the Foreign Office's devoting sufficient resources to enable sufficient representation there.

207. "The fluctuating frontier of Russia in Asia." *Nineteenth Century* 25 (February 1889): 267–83.

Claims that the present Russian frontier from the Caspian to Chinese Mongolia is an "artificial and temporary one" and is seen as such by the Russians. Russia is inexorably expanding and "may convulse two continents and embroil two nations." The frontier is analyzed in more detail and the British government encouraged to tell the Russians "thus far and no further."

208. "The history of Holwell's monument." *Bengal Past and Present* 15: 11–24.

History of the monument raised to Zephaniah Holwell and the other Europeans who were imprisoned in the "Black Hole of Calcutta" in 1756 and which Curzon undertook to restore.

209. "The House of Lords (No. 1): an unfair penalty on peers." *Nineteenth Century* 35 (April 1894): 525–37.

Article by Curzon, St. John Brodrick, and W.W. Palmer, all the eldest sons of peers, pressing the case for removing the "legal disability of peers on succeeding to their titles in respect of sitting in the House of Commons." A bill to this effect was defeated in Parliament.

210. "The Karun River and the commercial geography of south-west Persia. *Proceedings of the Royal Geographical Society.*" 12 (September 1890): 1–24.

Describes his travels in the Karun River region of Persia and stresses the importance of opening the river to British trade.

211. *The Kedleston Series. Vol. 1. Kedleston Church. An account, historical, descriptive and archaeological. By the Marquess Curzon (assisted by Murray Kendall).* London: Chiswick Press, 1922. 131.

History of the church from the 12th century based on Curzon family papers and other sources. Two further volumes were planned on Kedleston Hall and estate but were not completed.

212. *The Pamirs and the source of the Oxus. . . . With map and illustrations. Revised, and reprinted from* The Geographical Journal, *[vol. 8 (July 1896) 15, (August 1896) 97, (September 1896) 239.] etc.*

Account of his travels in the Pamir range which won for him the gold medal of the Royal Geographical Society. It provided him with an opportunity to indulge in the descriptive writing he enjoyed. In the Hunza valley nature showed herself "in the same moment tender and savage, radiant and appalling, the relentless spirit that hovers above the ice-towers and the gentle patroness of the field and orchard." But the work also included a history of earlier expeditions to the region with scholarly comments on its geography and geology.

213. *The personal history of Walmer Castle and its lords warden by the Marquess Curzon of Kedleston K.G.* Edited by Stephen Gwynn. London: Macmillan, 1927. 344.

An anecdotal history of the castle and its occupants from the time of the Duke of Dorset (1708–65) to the Duke of Wellington (1815–52), with a further chapter taking the story down to the First World War. The book is based on notes and drafts left by Curzon.

214. "The Queen Victoria Memorial Hall in India." *Nineteenth Century and After* 49 (June 1901): 949–59.

Explaining the thinking behind the Memorial Hall project, justifying its location in Calcutta rather than in Delhi, and describing the type of contents being sought for display in it: sculpture, paintings, engravings, treaties, and other documents, etc., representative of the history of British India.

215. "The reconstruction of the House of Lords: 'modus operandi.' " *National Review* 11 (April 1888): 153–75.

Follow up to his earlier article (no. 156 above) on the need for reform of the House of Lords. He now sets out his views on how the size of the upper chamber could be reduced, the incompetent members eliminated, able representatives brought in, and the hereditary system "purified."

216. "The referendum (No. II)." *National Review* 23 (March 1894): 72–76.

Opposes the use of the referendum in Britain to decide issues such as Irish home rule.

217. "The Rhey sculptures." *Athenaeum* 2 July 1893: 39.

Description of the ruined city of Shahr Rey, capital of Persia until the 13th century, and located some six miles south of Teheran.

218. "The 'scientific frontier' as accomplished fact." *Nineteenth Century* 23 (June 1888): 901–17.

His first article on the Indian frontier question in which he extols the steps that had been taken in recent years to strengthen India's northern defenses in the face of parliamentary criticism of the expenditure involved.

219. "The valley of waterfalls." *Macmillan's Magazine* 58 (July 1888): 184–91. (Reprinted in no. 200 above).

Vivid account of the scenery in the Yosemite Valley in California from his travels in 1887–88.

220. "The voice of Memnon." *Edinburgh Review* (July 1886): 263–83.

Account of the Aissaouia dervishes at the Tanner's Gate, Kairwan, Tunisia.

221. *Travels with a superior person.* Edited by Peter King. London: Sidgwick and Jackson, 1985. 191.

Follow-up to *A viceroy's India* (no. 159 above). This selection of Curzon's travel writings derives from his visits 1882–94 to lands other than India and all come from his *Tales of travel, Leaves from a viceroy's note-book,* and *Russia in central Asia.* The emphasis is on Curzon as a travel writer, and stories of ·overtly political importance have not been considered.

222. "Two demagogues: a parallel and a moral." *New Review* 12 (April 1895): 363–72.

Despite their different backgrounds, compares the careers of Lord Randolph Churchill and Joseph Chamberlain. Both have all the qualities of demagogues which, at the same time, make them unfit for leadership. However, Chamberlain is worthy of ministerial office. "For no man in England is capable of better and more useful work so long as he is driven and is not on any account allowed to drive." The article is signed by "Z" whom J.L. Garvin, in his *Life of Chamberlain*. vol. 2, p. 629, identified as Curzon. See also no. 203 above.

223. *War poems and other translations by Lord Curzon of Kedleston*. London: John Lane, 1915. 221.

Translations by Curzon of poems by the Belgian poet Emile Cammaerts and others mainly relating to the sufferings of the people of Belgium during the First World War with proceeds going to the Belgian Relief Fund.

224. "Wrestling in Japan." *New Review* 1 (September 1888): 395–408.
Account of Sumo wrestling from his travels in Japan.

225. "Young Conservatism." *National Review* 47 (January 1887): 577–87.
Written following Liberal attacks on the divided state of the Tory party and its lack of policies. Curzon stresses the growing number of young Conservatives with new ideas—such as reform of the House of Lords and the Church—and distances himself from the Tories of the past.

2. Introductions by Curzon

226. Carruthers, Douglas. *Unknown Mongolia. A record of travel and exploration in north-west Mongolia and Dzungaria*. London: Hutchinson, 1913. 2 vols. 659.

Curzon's preface raises the question of the future of "these mysterious regions." He sees the Mongolian tribesmen "now turning to the risen Sun of Russia to find a warmth and a protection which Chinese suzerainty has failed to give them."

227. Merewether, Lt. Col. John Walter Beresford and Sir Frederick Edwin Smith. *The Indian Corps in France*. London: John Murray, 1917. 550.

Described by Curzon as an "important and thrilling narrative of the deeds of the Indian Corps in France in the early days of the Great War." His introduction avoids any reference to his dispute with Kitchener over "dual control" of the Indian Army and any results of the outcome on the performance of the army in the war. He disputes any assertion, however, that the Indian Army was equipped by training to fight only in India.

228. Morier, James J. *The adventures of Haji Baba of Ispahan*. London: Macmillan, 1895. 456.

Curzon's 24-page introduction to Morier's fictional and satirical adventures of a Persian rogue includes an account of the historical background to Anglo-Persian relations.

228a. Oxford University. *Principles and methods of university reform. Report of the Hebdomadal Council. With an introduction submitted on behalf of the Council by Lord Curzon of Kedleston, chancellor of the univerity*. Oxford: Clarendon Press, 1910. 98.

Curzon sets out his reasons for the reforms and the importance of achieving them from within to pre-empt any attempt to impose unacceptable changes on the university from outside. The university's role as the imperial training ground must be preserved. The report includes the findings of various working parties set up at his instigation to look into reform of the university's constitution, faculties, entrance exams and admission policy, scholarships, etc.

3. Drafts Intended for Publication

All the following can be found among Curzon's papers in the India Office Library and Records.

229.   Essay on George Canning as foreign secretary (MSS. Eur. F112/607).

230.   Irish Home Rule Bill: unpublished article on (MSS. Eur. F112/604) 1886.

231.   On the Indian frontier. Manuscript for book vetoed on his appointment as viceroy; stopped at proof stage 1898 (MSS. Eur. F111/121).

Largely based on his 1894 travels in the Pamirs and the North-West Frontier region of India, but including comments on past and present policy which led Lord Salisbury to insist on his dropping the project.

4. Speeches

The following selection includes only published speeches. The main source for Curzon's other public speaking engagements is the press where they were widely covered (see chapter 5 below). For his speeches in Parliament see *Hansard's parliamentary debates* and reportage in *The Times.*

232.   *Address by Earl Curzon of Kedleston on the unveiling of the memorial to the late Earl of Cromer in Westminster Abbey, on Wednesday, the 12th. day of May, 1920. In Memorial to the late Earl of Cromer. Report to the contributors.* London: H.R. Stokes, 1920. 16.

Eulogistic review of Cromer's life concentrating on his work in Egypt where his recipe for success, "light taxation of the peasantry and the contentment of the governed," Curzon had employed in India.

233.   *Address delivered . . . by Lord Curzon . . . to the Trucial chiefs of the Arab Coast, at a public durbar held at Shargah on the 21st November 1903.* Printed in India: Foreign and Political Department. Treaties and engagements in force on 1st January 1906 between the British Government and the trucial chiefs of the Arab Coast, 1906. 4.

Speech by Curzon during his viceregal tour of the Persian Gulf in November 1903 to a gathering of rulers of the Gulf states stressing to them the benefits of British control of the region. "We saved you from extinction ·at the hands of your neighbours. We opened these seas to the ships of all nations and enabled their flags to fly in peace. We have not seized or held your territory. We have not destroyed your independence, but have preserved it.''

234. *Ancient monuments in India. Address of His Excellency Baron Curzon of Kedleston, at the annual meeting of the Asiatic Society of Bengal, 7th. February, 1900.* Reprinted from the *Proceedings of the Asiatic Society of Bengal* (1900). 12.

Curzon sets out the obligations of the government to preserve the ancient buildings of India.

235. *A recent journey in Afghanistan. A lecture delivered to the Royal Institution of Great Britain, 10 May 1895.* London: William Clowes and Sons, 1895. 12.

Account of his visit to Afghanistan in 1894 and his audiences with the Amir. Curzon is convinced of the Amir's goodwill toward the British to whom he looks for help in the defense of Afghan freedom.

236. *Clive memorial speech delivered in the Great Hall of Merchant Taylors' School on Friday, December 13th., 1907 . . . on the occasion of the unveiling of a mural tablet to the memory of Robert, Lord Clive.* 1907. 11.

Clive was one of the "master spirits of the English race" whose contribution to the development of British India was crucial. Curzon refutes any criticism of Clive on the grounds of self-seeking—his vision was much nobler and greater than that. In his description of Clive's "high ideal of duty" Curzon might even be talking of himself, and the speech is interesting in the other ways in which Curzon appears to identify himself with Clive.

237. *East and West.* 1911.

Printed version of Curzon's Glasgow University rectorial address taking the history of relations between Europe and Asia as its theme.

238. *Frontiers. The Romanes Lecture 1907. Delivered in the Sheldonian Theatre, Oxford, November 2, 1907.* Oxford: Clarendon Press, 1907. 58.

Stresses the "overwhelming influence of frontiers in the history of the modern world" and cites examples of wars arising from frontier disputes. He discusses different types of borders (natural, artificial, etc.) and different types of dependencies (protectorates, spheres of influence, etc.) and his own policy as viceroy of trying to maintain a ring of buffer states round India.

239. *Germany's move and Britain's answer. Speech by the Right Hon. Earl Curzon of Kedleston. On December 19th, 1916.* London: Hayman, Christy and Lilly, 1916. 18.

Speech to the House of Lords introducing the new War Cabinet's program and justifying its composition and reduced size. Asquith's government was a great success (e.g., its victory at the Somme, the introduction of national service, etc.) but there would be value in having a government drawing on the best talent available in both parties.

240. *Indian constitutional reform: speeches delivered in the House of Lords on October 23rd. and 24th. 1918, by the Marquess of Lansdowne, the Earl of Selborne, Lord Sydenham, Lord Macdonald and Earl Curzon.* London: Indo-British Association, 1918. 34.

Curzon, Selborne, and others opposed Midleton's proposal for a committee to consider Indian constitutional reform on the grounds that it would add tenfold to the problems of the Indian government during the war.

241. *Indian speeches of Lord Curzon [1896–1901].* Compiled by S.C. Sinha. Calcutta: Sanyal and Co., 1900, 1902. 2 vols.

Selection of Curzon's speeches as viceroy.

242. "Indiens Stelling im britischen Weltreich. Ein Vortrag gehalten von Lord Curzon of Kedleston vor der Philophischen Gefellfchaft in Edinburgh an 1 October 1909." *Koloniale Abhandlungen* 34–35 (1910). 29.

German translation of no. 260 below.

243. *Lord Curzon aux Indes: selection de ses discours comme viceroi et gouverneur-general de l'Inde 1899–1905. Introduction by Sir Thomas Raleigh.* Translation by Princesse F. de Faucigny-Lucinge. Paris, ?1906.

French translation of no. 244 below.

244. *Lord Curzon in India: being a selection from his speeches as viceroy and governor-general of India, 1898–1905. With a portrait, explanatory notes and an index, and with an introduction by Sir Thomas Raleigh.* London: Macmillan and Co., 1906. 640.

Standard edition of Curzon's speeches as viceroy.

245. *Lord Curzon's farewell to India: being speeches delivered . . . during Sept.–Nov. 1905 . . . Edited with an introduction, occasional notes and essays on certain aspects of his viceroyalty, by R.P. Karkaria.* Bombay: Thacker, 1907. 35.

Selection of Curzon's last speeches in India illustrating his "sympathy with the people of this country and an interest in their present state and future prospects."

246. *Lord Curzon's first and last speeches in India 1898–1905 . . .* Reprinted from the *Times of India.* Bombay: Times of India, 1905. 50.

Reprint of Curzon's inaugural and final speeches as viceroy. In the latter he claims to have the whole country and the bulk of the Indian Army behind him over his resignation. India will be his judge.

247. *Lord Curzon's justification of the Delhi Durbar.* [A speech delivered in the Imperial Legislative Council at Simla, 5 Sept. 1902, published as an appendix to no. 404 below.]

Curzon's arguments in favor of holding a durbar to mark the accession of Edward VII despite the expense, etc., involved. The durbar will break down the "water-tight compartment system" that characterizes the princely states and even the provinces within the Government of India.

248. *Modern parliamentary eloquence, The Rede lecture, delivered before the University of Cambridge, November 6, 1913.* London: Macmillan, 1913. 79.

Curzon traces the development of parliamentary speaking and regrets the declining use of classical quotation. He believes that the form of a speech is as important as its content.

249. *Notable speeches of Lord Curzon. With an introduction by H.K. Beauchamp . . . .* Edited by C. S. Raghunatha Rao. Madras: Arya Press, 1905. 435.

Important speeches made by Curzon as viceroy selected as "an almost perfect epitome of Lord Curzon's many-sided activities." Never before has a viceroy been so frank and open about policy matters in his public speeches.

250. *Oratio cancellarii ad admissionem.* Oxford, 1907.

Speech on conferment of chancellorship of Oxford University. [In Latin and English.]

251. *Path of honour . . . speech delivered by Earl Curzon of Kedleston at a meeting at the Mansion House, London on behalf of the National Committee for Relief in Belgium.* Undated. 7.

Fund-raising speech on behalf of Belgian war relief.

252. *Persian autonomy. Speech delivered by the Rt. Hon. Earl Curzon of Kedleston at the inaugural dinner of the Persia Society at the Savoy Hotel, London, on 15th November 1911.* London: Persia Society, 1912. 11.

It is essential for Britain that Persia has a strong government. Britain should be prepared to assist toward this end.

253. *Speech by the viceroy, Lord Curzon, concluding the budget debate in the Legislative Council on 22 March 1905.* Calcutta, 1905.

Speech in justification of his budget.

254. *Speech delivered by Lord Curzon of Kedleston in the debate on the second reading of the Finance Bill, in the House of Lords, November 30, 1909.* London: National Union of Conservative and Constitutional Associations, 1909. 16.

Opposes various aspects of the Bill, particularly the threat to the House of Lords. The second chamber must not be rendered "impotent and ridiculous by the paralysis of its powers."

255. *Speeches by Lord Curzon of Kedleston, viceroy and governor-general of India.* Calcutta: Government of India, 1900–6. 4 vols. 1512.

Official edition of his speeches as viceroy, including his visit to England in 1904.

256. *Speeches by Lord Curzon of Kedleston, viceroy and governor-general of India 1898–1901*. Calcutta: Thacker, Spink and Co., 1901. 455.

Speeches delivered before his departure from England in 1898 and in India 1898–1901 covering such topics as famine, ancient monuments, and the Victoria Memorial Hall.

257. *Speeches delivered during a visit to the Southport division of south-west Lancashire in December, 1891, by Hon. Geo. N. Curzon, M.P.) (under-secretary of state for India), and republished from the* Southport Visitor. Southport: Johnson and Co., ?1891/92. 87.

Reporting Curzon's speeches on the rural question, Ireland, temperance, leasehold enfranchisement, etc.

258. *Speeches on India delivered by Lord Curzon . . . while in England in July–August, 1904*. London: John Murray, 1904. 51.

Text of four speeches by Curzon at the Guildhall, Mansion House, borough of Derby and the United Club covering various aspects of his viceroyalty.

259. *Subjects of the day: being a collection of speeches and writings by Lord Curzon of Kedleston. With an introduction by the Earl of Cromer*. Edited by Desmond M. Chapman-Huston. London: George Allen and Unwin, 1915. 439.

Selection of speeches mainly on the empire, India, domestic affairs (including "Women's work," and "The power of the press"), foreign countries, personal tributes (including George Wyndham and Lord Roberts), national service, women's suffrage, and the First World War.

260. *The place of India in the Empire. Being an address delivered before the Philosophical Institute of Edinburgh . . . on October 19, 1909*. London: John Murray, 1909. 46.

India has become the strategic center of the defensive position of the British Empire and can no longer be regarded as being "somewhat outside the main congeries of States and communities that compose the Empire."

261. *The true imperialism . . . an address delivered in the Town Hall, Birmingham, on Wednesday, December 11th. 1907*. Birmingham: Birmingham and Midland Institute, 1907. 24.

Full-blown exposition of Curzon's imperial philosophy, including his views on the moral basis of imperialism; widely reported in the press, including *The Times*, which regarded it as "masterly."

262. *The war. A speech delivered in Harrow Speech Room on October 14th, 1914, etc*. London: Victoria League, 1914. 12.

Spells out German aims and ambitions from the War and exhorts the full support of his audience. He lists ways in which people should behave to encourage the war effort, including patient acceptance if the war drags on, support for the government, and tolerance as the casualty lists begin to lengthen.

5. Editions

263.   *1898–1905. The Lord Curzon of Kedleston. Correspondence with Victoria and Edward VII, secretaries of state, persons in India and abroad, and others.* Government of India, 35 vols., undated.

Prints Curzon's official viceregal correspondence with the royal family, government ministers, and others.

264.   *Correspondence with Right Hon. St. John Brodrick M.P. In England: India Office correspondence with the secretary of state for India . . . and the viceroy of India.* 1903, 1906.

265.   Farrington, Anthony (editor). *Lord Curzon's Japan diaries.* Annotated by Roger Machin. Nagoya, Japan: Richard Cocks Society, 1985. 127.

Publishes the text of Curzon's diaries relating to his visits to Japan during his world tours of 1887–88 and 1892–93, with footnotes in English and Japanese.

266.   Oxford University. *Correspondence between a committee of Merton College and Lord Curzon of Kedleston . . . concerning the financial administration of the college.* Oxford, 1909.

6. Members of Curzon's Family

267.   Bradley, John (editor). *Lady Curzon's India. Letters of a vicereine.* London: Weidenfeld and Nicolson, 1985. 180.

Publishes a selection of Mary Curzon's letters to her husband and family, mainly from India, with extracts from her Indian travel diary (Hyderabad in 1902 and the Persian Gulf in 1903); concludes with Curzon's letter to Mrs. Leiter describing Mary Curzon's death.

268.   Curzon, Grace, Marchioness. *Reminiscences.* London: Hutchinson, 1955. 256.

Interesting for the light they throw on Curzon's personality, but little on his official career in which she took little interest. Nobody was indifferent to Curzon: he was either liked or disliked. He was a most complicated person: easily hurt and easily pleased, perfectionist and fussy over detail, naturally dignified but not pompous. She claims credit for preventing Curzon resigning from Lloyd George's government over his meddling in foreign policy as she realized his obsessive need for work. She contributes nothing new to the issue of sucession to the premiership after Law's resignation. There is much on the social side of her life as wife of the foreign secretary and on her family by an earlier marriage.

B. BIOGRAPHICAL AND HISTORICAL STUDIES

1. General

269. Anstruther, Ian. *Oscar Browning: a biography.* London: John Murray, 1983. 209.

Biography of Eton master and historian whose relationship with Curzon at Eton led to his dismissal in 1875. Little new evidence is produced on the nature of this and other relationships Browning had with boys at the college, but a chapter entitled "Greek love and George Curzon" attempts to analyze Browning's feelings for his protégés. There is an entertaining account of Browning's visit to India in 1902 when he was entertained in style by Curzon.

270. Blake, Robert, Lord Blake. *The unknown prime minister. The life and times of Andrew Bonar Law 1858–1923.* London: Eyre and Spottiswoode, 1955. 556.

Useful for the light it throws on Curzon's position in the Conservative Opposition camp before the War and his part in the replacement of Asquith's coalition government by Lloyd George's ministry. The author also provides an important account, based on the papers in the Royal Archives, of Law's resignation as premier in 1923 and the choice of Baldwin as successor in preference to Curzon. Law would appear not to have been instrumental in Baldwin's choice.

271. Brett, Maurice and Oliver Brett (editors). *Journals and letters of Reginald, Viscount Esher, 1870–1930. London: 1934–38.* 4 vols.

Throws light on Curzon's conflict with Kitchener in India.

272. Browning, Oscar. *Memories of later years.* London: T. Fisher Unwin Ltd., 1923. 223.

Supplementary to his earlier *Memories of sixty years* (2nd. edition, 1910) and includes an account of his trip to India in 1902 to visit Curzon; of mainly anecdotal interest. Browning basks in the reflected glory of his most successful pupil who assured him that he had "greater power than any European sovereign, that he was allowed a free hand by the Indian secretary provided that he kept him well informed of what he proposed to do and that they were on excellent terms." (p. 68).

273. Chapman-Huston, D. "The orator and the man." *New Criterion* (April 1926): 313–28.

Memoir of Curzon stressing his many gifts in addition to his talents as a public speaker.

274. Churchill, Randolph S. *Winston S. Churchill. Volume 1. Youth 1874–1900.* London: Heinemann, 1966. 608. *Companion* Part 1 1874–1896 and Part 2 1896–1900. London: Heinemann, 1967. 1290.

First volume in monumental biographical series with companion volumes of illustrative documents. Having considered Curzon initially a "superior Oxford prig" Churchill is completely won over during a visit to India. "He is a remarkable man—and to my surprise I found he had great charm of manner . . . I think his viceroyalty will be a great success." (Vol. 1, p. 436).

275. ———. *Winston S. Churchill. Volume 2. Young statesman 1901–1914.* London: Heinemann, 1967. 775. *Companion* Part 1 1901–7, Part 2 1907–11 and Part 3 1911–14. London: Heinemann, 1969. 2159.

Like the earlier volumes in the series important in charting the developing relationship between the future Cabinet colleagues, Curzon and Churchill. Churchill supports Curzon's stance against Kitchener in India. "What has happened is that the Commander-in-Chief has not merely swallowed up his own War Minister but the Viceroy as well" (Vol. 2, p. 95). Churchill also refers in passing to Curzon's position on such issues as women's suffrage and the constitutional crisis of 1910.

For subsequent volumes in this series, see under Gilbert, Martin.

276. Churchill, Sir Winston S. *Great contemporaries.* London: Thornton Butterworth Ltd, 1937. 335.

A series of essays on Asquith, Curzon, Morley, Rosebery, Clemenceau, Hindenburg, and other important figures who "shone" at the turn of the century. The volume includes a perceptive picture of Curzon: "Here was a being gifted far beyond the average level . . . and yet who failed to achieve the central purpose of his life." Among his weaknesses Churchill points to his lack of political guile (e.g., allowing Kitchener to out-maneuver him in India, and agreeing to serve as Baldwin's foreign secretary in 1923 when a refusal to do so would probably have brought him the premiership after the disastrous 1923 election campaign). "Bespangled with every quality that could dazzle and attract, he never found himself with a following. Majestic in speech, appearance and demeanour, he never led. He often domineered, but at the centre he never dominated."

277. Dugdale, Blanche E. C. *Arthur James Balfour First Earl of Balfour, K.G., O.M., F.R.S., Etc.* London: Hutchinson and Co, 1936, 2 vols. 898.

Includes a chapter on Balfour's involvement as prime minister in the Curzon-Kitchener controversy, quoting correspondence between Curzon and Balfour and the latter's reports to the king. Balfour tries hard to stay on good terms with the viceroy despite his opposition to Curzon's expansionist foreign policy and his sympathy with the tenor of Kitchener's military proposals; however, what is seen as Curzon's increasingly unreasonable and neurotic behavior makes a rupture with Balfour's government inevitable. On Curzon's foreign secretaryship the author feels that Balfour would never have stood for the amount of interference from Lloyd George that Curzon had to cope with, but concedes that Balfour's indolence at the Foreign Office in the period immediately before this allowed Lloyd George to establish a foothold. Balfour, himself, felt Curzon exaggerated the case: "It's the rarest thing . . . when the Prime Minister and the Foreign

Minister don't clash. That's what makes me so impatient of all this talk about Lloyd George interfering so much. I don't say Lloyd George didn't often do things he had better not have. But you can't expect the P.M. not to interfere with Foreign Office business" (Vol. 2, pp. 292–93). There is disappointingly little on Balfour's role in the choice of a successor to Law as premier in 1923.

278. Dundas, John L., Earl of Ronaldshay. *The life of Lord Curzon. Being the authorized biography of George Nathaniel Marquess Curzon of Kedleston, K.G.* London: Ernest Benn Ltd., 1928, 3 vols. 1199.

Remains the most definitive study of Curzon's life based on personal knowledge, information supplied by Lady Curzon, Malcolm, Midleton, and others who knew Curzon well, and on Curzon's own extensive archive of private papers as well as on his correspondence with contemporaries. Each volume deals with a period of his career. The author's main concern is with Curzon's official career, and although his personal life receives some mention his relationship with his family and other close associates such as the Souls is not explored in any depth. Volume one covers his education at Eton and Balliol, his entry into politics, under-secretaryships, travels, writings, and his appointment as viceroy. In describing the development of Curzon's political views much use is made of his contributions to contemporary journals and reviews. Ronaldshay attempts to analyze Curzon's personality and character as from these crucial formative years he "displayed symptoms of a very complex personality, and it is during these early years that can best be studied those conflicting elements in his temperament and character that often made him so difficult to understand" (Vol. 1, pp. 3–4).

The whole of the second volume is devoted to Curzon's viceroyalty. Curzon regarded India as the scene of his greatest triumphs and in giving over so much space to this period of his career the author feels he is reflecting Curzon's wishes. "For it was in India, he believed, if the full story of his Administration was ever told, that he might be held by his fellow men to have laboured not altogether in vain" (Vol. 2, p. 4). The volume includes a detailed and authoritative account of Curzon's viceroyalty with particularly helpful sections on his foreign policy and his administrative reforms. Ronaldshay is generally sympathetic to Curzon's position in issues such as "dual control" where, in particular, Curzon's stance had been vindicated by later events. In analyzing Curzon's difficulties with Kitchener, Balfour, Midleton, and others the temperament and personality of each undoubtedly played an important part, but a franker assessment is impaired by the proximity of events. "That many of Lord Curzon's communications were characterised by considerable asperity of language is undoubtedly the case; but his attitude in this respect cannot be fairly judged except in the light of the nature and extent of the provocation which he received" (Vol. 2, p. 403). Curzon's shortcomings, such as his inability to take account of the growth of Indian nationalism, are touched on, but "the verdict of history will assuredly be that great as his Viceroyalty was, judged merely by the nature and extent of its legislative and administrative achievements, it was infinitely greater by reason of the exalted standards of duty and honour by which it was inspired'' (Vol. 2. p. 421).

Volume three provides a balanced account of Curzon's public offices after his return from India and his other activities such as his chancellorship of Oxford University, restoration of historic buildings, and presidency of the Royal Geographical Society. Ronaldshay feels Curzon showed ''amazing courage'' in occupying government office for the last ten years of his life almost continuously despite constant physical pain and the disappointing end to his viceroyalty. After reviewing the events of Curzon's foreign secretaryship in some detail the author feels that it did not live up to expectations. This is put down to Curzon's inability to play second fiddle to Lloyd George in foreign policy, his interest in planning policy but not in implementing it, and his unsuitability for the post-war world where ''the qualities which the British Foreign Minister had now to cultivate were those, not of enterprise and daring, but of endless patience, never-failing equanimity and tact'' (Vol. 3, p. 367). The approach is necessarily biographical and the author is more concerned with Curzon's motives and the effect of events on him. He feels that a fully objective assessment of Curzon's foreign secretaryship will have to wait until the dust of the controversies of the 1920s has subsided.

279.   Egremont, Max. *A life of Arthur James Balfour.* London: Collins, 1980. 391.

Like Dugdale above, defends Balfour's role in the Curzon-Kitchener dispute. Curzon was his own worst enemy. ''An extraordinary hysteria had entered into his behaviour and this, combined with ill health and self-pity, resulted in self-delusion . . .'' (p. 174). Curzon's part in persuading Balfour not to oppose the Parliament Bill in 1911 is emphasized. Some light is also thrown on Balfour's role in 1923 in advising the king against choosing Curzon as prime minister.

280.   ———. *The cousins: the friendship, opinions and activities of Wilfred Scawen Blunt and George Wyndham.* London: Collins, 1977. 320.

Interesting for the light it throws on Curzon's private life. An important source is Curzon's personal correspondence with George Wyndham and Sibell, Lady Grosvenor. The latter married Wyndham but only after a romantic involvement with Curzon in the 1880s. There is also much interesting background on the all-male Crabbet Club of which Blunt, Curzon, and Wyndham were prominent members.

281.   Faber, Richard. *The vision and the need: late Victorian imperialist aims.* London: Faber and Faber, 1966. 150.

This review of Victorian imperialism includes a discussion of Curzon's imperialist philosophy and compares it with the views of other contemporary advocates of British expansionism such as Cromer and Milner.

282.   Feiling, Keith. *Sketches in nineteenth century biography.* London: Longmans, Green and Co, 1930. 181.

A selection of biographical essays, first published in *The Times*, includes statesmen such as Pitt, Canning, Disraeli, and Curzon. The Curzon sketch concentrates on Lord Ronaldshay's *Life* (no. 278 above), volumes one and two of which Feiling considers exemplary. However, volume three covering Curzon's political career after his return from India is less satisfactory. Curzon's standpoint on issues such as Ireland and women's suffrage are not always clearly delineated and often come over as contradictory. More information is needed on Curzon's views. In the earlier volumes we get to know the man, but he emerges as something of an enigma in Ronaldshay's later sections. Feiling does not necessarily regard Curzon as a failure. He paved the way in India for many of the advances made in the twentieth century. "... he was one of the ancien regime who unwittingly make change inevitable; who so hew and break the ground, that crops they have not sown spring up in the clean soil" (p. 159).

283. Gardiner, A.G. *Prophets, priests and kings.* London: Alston Rivers Ltd, 1908. 332.

Series of biographical sketches, first published in the *Daily News*, covers a wide range of figures prominent in public life. With Curzon appear John Burns, Florence Nightingale, the Kaiser, G.B. Shaw, and Mrs Pankhurst. Gardiner concentrates on Curzon's Indian career where he finds much to criticize. Curzon's "grandiose vision of himself as Caesar was at the root of most of his mistakes in India," including "that stupendous white elephant, the Victoria memorial" (of which Curzon was in fact extremely proud). The money gathered for the memorial might have been more appropriately spent encouraging the development of Indian industry. Curzon's "contempt" for Indians is held largely responsible for the growth of the Indian nationalist movement. However, Curzon's energy and commitment are recognized, and his viceroyalty did produce much-needed reforms in areas such as education.

284. Gilbert, Martin. *Winston S. Churchill. Volume 3. 1914–1916.* London: Heinemann, 1971. 988. *Companion* Part 1 July 1914–April 1915, Part 2 May 1915–December 1916.

Both the main volume and its companions shed light on Curzon's membership in the War Cabinet, particularly his views on the Dardanelles campaign and the conscription issue over which he joined other members of the government in a plot to engineer Kitchener's removal from the War Office in October 1915. The volumes also document Curzon's role in preventing Churchill from joining the coalition government formed in 1916.

285. ———. *Winston S. Churchill. Volume 4. 1916–1922.* London: Heinemann, 1975. 967. *Companion* Part 1 January 1917–June 1919, Part 2 July 1919–March 1921, Part 3 April 1921–November 1922. London: Heinemann, 1977. 2165.

Further material is included to illustrate Curzon's opposition to Churchill's inclusion in the government. Curzon told Lloyd George: "He is a potential danger in opposition. In the opinion of all of us he will as a member of the Govt. be an active danger in our midst.'' There is much on the relations between Curzon and Churchill in the years 1919–20 over British involvement in the Russian civil war and in connection with Churchill's Middle and Far Eastern policy as colonial secretary from 1921. Curzon resented Churchill's interference in negotiations with Japan over renewal of the 1902 treaty, writing to his wife of Churchill's attempts to ''be a sort of Asiatic Foreign Secretary.'' These issues are extensively documented in the three companion volumes.

286. ———. *Winston S. Churchill. Volume 5. 1922–1939*. London: Heinemann, 1976. 1167. *Companion Part 1. The Exchequer Years 1922–1929*. London: Heinemann, 1979. 1504.

Includes much less material on Curzon than the previous volumes but touches on Churchill's differences with him over foreign and naval policy. Churchill's opinion on Curzon's death: ''. . . he did not inspire affection, nor represent great causes.''

287. Glyn, Anthony. *Elinor Glyn. A biography*. London: Hutchinson, 1955. 356.

Biography of the novelist and film producer, Elinor Glyn, with whom Curzon had an affair from c.1908. Written by her grandson and based on her diaries it includes a charming account of her relationship with Curzon which began in the lonely years after the death of his first wife. Despite differences over issues such as women's suffrage the two remained close until Curzon entered the coalition government in 1915. He wrote over 200 letters to her in this period, all of which she destroyed following his engagement to Grace Hinds in the following year.

288. Goradia, Nayana. Forthcoming study of Curzon's psychology based on her earlier Calcutta University Ph.D.

289. Gwynn, S.L. *The letters and friendship of Sir Cecil Spring-Rice. A record*. London: Constable, 1929, 2 vols. 966.

Includes a number of comments on Curzon by Spring-Rice, a diplomat and close friend from their school days together at Eton. ''I am always in two minds about Curzon. He has a great deal of industry and courage and also sterling qualities, but it isn't a fine nature, and I sometimes wonder how much he prizes the thing and how much the show.''

290. Harmsworth, Cecil. *Immortals at first hand. Famous people as seen by their contemporaries*. London: Harmsworth, 1933. 254.

Collection of short, fairly light-weight, essays on prominent writers, politicians, and others by contemporaries. The Curzon sketch is wriiten by Harmsworth himself who finds him a ''puzzling and intriguing personality.'' He was the best-informed and most accomplished statesman of the day, but he was pompous and obsessively perfectionist. His manner and temperament deprived him of the premiership.

291.   Hogarth, David G. "George Nathaniel Curzon, Marquess Curzon of Kedleston, 1859–1925." Reproduced from *Proceedings of the British Academy* 11 (1924–25): 502–24.

Laudatory review of Curzon's life concentrating on his less well known contributions to exploration and geography, the preservation of Indian antiquities, his chancellorship of Oxford University, and presidency of the Royal Geographical Society.

292.   Hurd, Percy Angier (editor). *People you know being intimate portraits of some of the men and women of to-day.* Bristol: Arrowsmith, 1900. 317.

Series of anonymous pen portraits, originally printed in *The Outlook*, by "intimate friends" of the subjects. Curzon (pp. 136–42), Cecil Rhodes, Salisbury, and others receive light-hearted treatment. Curzon is not a "prig" but a "first class fighting man," who, once he has been fully accepted by the governing elite, will be recognized for the exceptionally talented individual that he is.

293.   Hutton, W.H. "Lord Curzon. The *Life*; and some memories." *Nineteenth Century and After* 621 (November 1928): 683–98.

Essentially a review of Lord Ronaldshay's *Life* (no. 278 above) which is taken to task for describing Curzon as more "malleable" in his later years and being prepared to accept faits accompli to please others. Hutton contends that Curzon can no longer be regarded as a "pompous man, or unsympathetic, or arrogant, or a poseur." There was a genuine "modesty" in his character that even Ronaldshay had not identified.

294.   Jones, Sir Clement. "Lord Curzon of Kedleston, 1859–1925: an appreciation." *International Affairs* 37.3 (July 1961): 332–38.

Memoir of Curzon based on Jones's personal knowledge and surviving letters to him from Curzon; of particular interest as Jones was secretary to the Shipping Control Committee in 1916 when Curzon was in charge. He later joined the Cabinet Secretariat when the War Cabinet was set up by Asquith. Jones's reminiscences touch on Curzon's unpredictability in his relations with staff, and on his consummate skills as an administrator.

295.   Judd, Denis. *Balfour and the British empire. A study in imperial evolution 1874–1932.* London: Macmillan, 1968. 392.

Provides a sympathetic treatment of Balfour's line over the Curzon-Kitchener affair. Curzon's "incapacity for objective self-analysis" led him to treat disagreement from London as treachery. Balfour's real grasp of the Indian situation may, as Curzon claimed, have been insubstantial although "metaphysically beautiful," but at least his arguments never rivalled Curzon's emotional and almost unbalanced diatribes (p. 250). Curzon's administrative reforms in India were overdue and worthwhile but he was responsible for pushing the nationalist movement toward extremism and therefore left the foundations of British rule in India weaker than he found them.

296.   Lambert, Angela. *Unquiet Souls. The Indian summer of the British aristocracy 1880–1918.* London: Macmillan, 1984. 262.

Popular account of the lives and affairs of the Souls. Of some interest for the background it provides on the lives of the members of this aristocratic coterie to which Curzon belonged, but lacks historical substance. Curzon's friend, the hostess Mary, Countess of Wemyss, is described as "generous, impulsive, unpunctual, unselfconscious, warmhearted, kind." Curzon's inter-relationship with other Souls, male and female, is explored, and some light thrown on his relations with his first and second wives, and with Elinor Glyn.

297.   Leslie, Sir John R.S. *Studies in sublime failure.* London: Ernest Benn, 1932. 295.

Studies of Cardinal Newman, C.S. Parnell, Curzon, and others. "When comparison is made with any such character in antiquity, the note of failure becomes uppermost in Curzon." His moodiness, unpredictability, megalomania, and other traits added up to a flawed character which lay at the root of his failures. "Brilliance and paradox" were not what the popular mind wanted to see in a post-war prime minister.

298.   Malcolm, Sir Ian Zachary. "George Curzon." *Quarterly Review* 245 (July 1925): 1–22.

Revealing character sketch by a politician and diplomat who had been private secretary to both Salisbury and Balfour and who formed a life-long friendship with Curzon, being named as his executor.

299.   Mosley, Leonard O. *Curzon. The end of an epoch.* London: Longman, 1960. 301.

Intended not as a political biography in a narrow sense but as a study of the whole "complex and temperamental" man: his psychology and his public and private life (p. xii). His unhappy relationship with his second wife and grown-up children, and colleagues like Kitchener, whose conduct Curzon was "naive, ingenuous and lacking in perception" not to predict (p. 103), and Lloyd George, who became "bored by his verbosity, suspicious of his loyalty, and tolerant of him only as long as he believed . . . that Curzon commanded the influence of the Tory Party" (p. 209), are examined.

300.   Nicolson, Harold. "I knew a man." *The Listener* (21 April 1937): 737–39.

Popular sketch of Curzon's career by his former Foreign Office colleague and biographer.

301.   ———. "George Nathaniel Curzon, Marquess Curzon of Kedleston (1859–1925)." *Dictionary of National Biography 1922–1930.* London: Oxford University Press, 1937. 221–34.

Balanced summary of Curzon's career in public life, drawing largely on Ronaldshay's *Life* (no. 278 above) but with frank assessments of his achievements and failures. Curzon's spinal injury is blamed for "that lack of elasticity that hampered his splendid activities of mind and soul" but there is little doubt that he had a "natural tendency to self-pity" which could lead to exaggeration of his condition. The main issues of Curzon's terms of office in India and at the Foreign Office are clearly described, and the inconsistencies in his behavior over Ireland and women's suffrage touched upon. Over all, Curzon "achieved successes rather than success." He failed to triumph "over his own anachronisms" and "to adapt himself to the needs of a transitional age which did not like him and which he did not like."

302. Raymond, E.T. *Uncensored celebrities*. London: T. Fisher Unwin, 1918. 244.

Biographical sketches reprinted from *The Everyman* of Balfour, Curzon, Churchill, and other politicians "designed to assist the process of revaluation" in the post war world. "There was never a stage in Lord Curzon's career when he did not promise more than he has actually performed." His success in India is the subject of debate, his contribution to the War Cabinet debatable. His travel writings reveal him "not only as a shrewd, if rather superficial, observer, but as the possessor of a quite complicated superiority, racial, social, and personal."

303. Rose, Kenneth. *Superior person. A portrait of Curzon and his circle in late Victorian England*. London: Weidenfeld and Nicolson, 1969. 475.

Study of Curzon concentrating on the development of his personality and outlook, his education, travels, and political career down to his appointment as viceroy in 1898. A concluding chapter carries the story forward through his viceroyalty and charts the main events of his later career. As the title suggests the author sets out to study Curzon against his background. He sees this as the last period in which control of public affairs is the preserve of an oligarcy of aristocratic and landowning families, when the "shared intimacies of Eton and Balliol, of country house and London club, continued to influence policy at home and abroad. It was still the age of gunroom diplomacy" (p. xiii). Rose is particularly successful in exploring the inter-relationship between Curzon and those individuals who most influenced his development or with whom he was closely associated in the course of his official career. These include Browning, Jowett, Salisbury, Brodrick, and Balfour. In terms of Curzon's official career this biography is thus less definitive than Ronaldshay's *Life* (no. 278 above), but in the information it provides about Curzon's private life it is much fuller and gives a much more rounded picture of the man. This is facilitated by extensive use of the private papers of contemporaries. These produce a plethora of revealing comments about Curzon by those who knew him best, although there is a tendency for this to become anecdotal in places, particularly where the extracts are already familiar from other secondary sources.

Some of the early episodes of Curzon's life have already been well charted and Rose's chapters on university life and the Souls contain little that is new. The sections on Curzon's travels in Central Asia, Persia, and the Pamirs are probably the best of those dealing with non-political themes. His under-secretaryship at the India Office receives disappointingly little coverage. However, his period at the Foreign Office under Salisbury is correctly appreciated for its importance in establishing Curzon's political reputation. There is detailed discussion both of the particular issues he had to deal with, as well as of his relations with Salisbury. He succeeded in maintaining a close working relationship for three years with Salisbury and in defending the latter's policies in the House of Commons despite being constantly frustrated by what he saw as a lack of assertiveness in Salisbury's approach to Britain's overseas commitments.

304. Sforza, Count Carlo. *Makers of modern Europe. Portraits and personal impressions and recollections.* Indianapolis: Bobbs-Merrill, 1930. 420.

Reminiscences of the former Italian foreign minister of European rulers and statesmen, including Curzon, encountered in the course of his life. The appointment as foreign secretary of a man of Curzon's background and attitudes "proves that we, on the European continent and in America, will never be able to fathom the mysteries and the guilelessness of English decisions." Curzon's failure to stand up to Lloyd George in foreign affairs, his failure to come to grips with the French mentality, particularly Poincaré, his lack of interest in seeing his policies through once he had completed the presentation of his case, all come in for criticism.

305. Sykes, Christopher. *Nancy. The life of Lady Astor.* London: Panther, 2nd. edition 1979 (1st. edition 1972). 637.

Interesting for Curzon's relationship with Waldorf Astor (of whom Balfour and Curzon were political mentors) and with Nancy Astor with whom Curzon conducted an unrestrained and flirtatious correspondence until his second marriage which he announced to her in a "majestically formal" letter.

306. Vincent, Edgar, Viscount d'Abernon. *Portraits and appreciations.* London: Hodder and Stoughton, 1931. 259.

Series of character sketches reprinted from his published *Diary* by Curzon's ambassador to Germany. He emphasizes the contradictions in Curzon's make-up ("his unique achievement was to combine pomposity with humour"), but is not as perceptive as other commentators in identifying flaws. He makes much of Curzon's "unremitting and indefatigable" service for his country. Curzon's disappointment over the premiership in 1923 resulted in his death soon after.

307. Wortham, Hugh E. *Oscar Browning.* London: Constable, 1927. 327.

Authorized biography of Browning including a chapter on "The Curzon Affair" which provides a sympathetic account of Browning's relationship with Curzon at Eton which derived solely from his recognition of Curzon's potential and a desire to further his intellectual development.

308. Wright, Peter E. *Portraits and criticisms.* London: Eveleigh Nash and Grayson, 1925. 214.

Selection of articles on such subjects as "Mr. Churchill and the war," "Mr. Lloyd George and his foreign policy," and "Lord Curzon's career." Curzon's real talents lie in writing rather than in politics to which he is unsuited. As foreign secretary "he works in order to write, and does not write in order to work." However, even the best of his books, such as *Tales of Travel* (no. 201 above), show his inability to sift the trivial from the important.

309. Zebel, Sydney Henry. *Balfour: a political biography.* Cambridge: Cambridge University Press, 1973. 312.

Includes material on Curzon's relationship with Balfour, with particular emphasis on the "dual control" controversy and Baldwin's appointment as premier in 1923.

2. Family Background and Early Years (1859–98)

310. Brereton, J.M. "Superior person and absolute amir." *Blackwood's Magazine* 324 (1978): 141–51.

Provides an account of Curzon's visit to Afghanistan in 1894 and of his meeting with the amir, Abd-er Rahman Khan.

311. Coleridge, Gilbert James Duke. *Eton in the Seventies.* London: Smith, Elder and Co., 1912. 293.

Background to Curzon's education at Eton, with much detail of his early precociousness, role in "Pop," talents as a public speaker, etc.

312. Curzon, Richard N., Viscount Scarsdale. *Kedleston Hall. An illustrated survey of the historic Derbyshire home of the Curzon family.* Derbyshire Countryside Ltd., 1958. 30.

Illustrated guide book to the house and its occupants.

313. Cust, Sir Lionel. "Eton vintage [1870–80.]" *Fortnightly Review* (October 1928): 496–503.

Includes references to Curzon at Eton.

314. Gillard, D.R. "Salisbury and the Indian defence problem, 1885–1902." In Kenneth Bourne and D.C. Watt (editors). *Studies in international history. Essays presented to W. Norton Medlicott.* London: Longmans, 1967. 236–48.

Discusses Salisbury's policies for the defense of India against Russian aggression: remain on good terms with the other Powers and prevent India's neighbors from becoming Russian bases. The study includes little of specific relevance to Curzon but important for its delineation of Salisbury's non-aggressive policies abroad against which Curzon felt so strongly.

315. Gosses, Frans. *The management of British foreign policy before the First World War, especially during the period 1880–1914.* Translated by E.C. van der Gaaf. Leiden: A.W. Sijthoff's Uitgeversmaat schappij N.V., 1948. 172.

Includes an assessment of Curzon as under-secretary at the Foreign Office: his success in getting access to Salisbury's private correspondence with British diplomats abroad and to visiting delegations, but his inability to ensure any real influence over Salisbury's decisions.

316. Kelly, J.B. "Salisbury, Curzon and the Kuwait Agreement of 1899." In Kenneth Bourne and D.C. Watt (editors). *Studies in International History. Essays presented to W. Norton Medlicott.* London: Longmans, 1967. 249–90.

Detailed account of the background to the agreement and Curzon's advocacy of Britain accepting Kuwait as a protectorate to strengthen the British position in the Gulf. Despite Salisbury's misgivings about committing Britain to this level of support the eventual agreement went further than he wished. Later events justified Curzon's success in achieving a greater degree of British involvement in the region.

317. Maclean, Sir Fitzroy H. *A person from England and other travellers.* London: Jonathan Cape, 1958. 384.

Account of nineteenth-century travellers in Turkestan, scene of a struggle for paramountcy (the "great game") between Britain and Russia. A chapter (entitled "Superior Person") describes Curzon's travels in the region in 1888 based on his published writings.

318. Ramm, Agatha. "Lord Salisbury and the Foreign Office." In Roger Bullen (editor). *The Foreign Office 1782–1982.* 46–65.

Background on Salisbury's control of foreign policy. He delegated details but retained overall control.

3. Viceroyalty (1898–1905)

319. Anonymous. "Lord Curzon and the Indian National Congress." *Calcutta Review* 131 (April 1954): 39–52.

Publishes private correspondence between Curzon and Lord George Hamilton on this question.

320. ———. "Lord Curzon and Tibet." *Public Opinion* 85 (1904): 567.

321. ———. "Native thinker. Lord Curzon and the native states." *Calcutta Review* 121 (July 1905): 398–407.

Contemporary discussion of Curzon's relations with the Indian princes.

322. ———. "Our future in Tibet." *Spectator* 93 (1904): 41.

Expresses reservations over Curzon's assertive policy toward Tibet lest Tibet becomes a British protectorate with the implications for future British involvement.

323. ———. "Our policy in Tibet." *North China Herald* 72 (1904): 242–43.

In opposition to Curzon's Tibetan policy.

324. ————. *Proceedings of a public meeting held at the Calcutta Town Hall on the 10th. March 1905. A protest against Lord Curzon's last convocation address and general administration.* Calcutta: Prithwis Chandra Ray, 1905. 34.
Account of proceedings of a public meeting condemning Curzon's Calcutta Municipal Act, the partition of Bengal etc.

325. ————. "The British case against Tibet." *Outlook* 78 (1904): 161–63.
Discusses Curzon's policy in Tibet based on *India under Lord Curzon* (no. 375 below).

326. ————. "The expedition into Tibet." *Spectator* 91 (1903): 857–58.
Article written in support of Curzon's forward policy in Tibet.

327. ————. *The failure of Lord Curzon.* 1903.
Anonymous pamphlet attacking Curzon's land revenue reforms on the grounds that his policy "was pushing the agricultural population lower and lower in the slough of misery." More generally his autocratic meddlesomeness in domestic affairs and imperialism abroad are also taken to task.

328. ————. "The men who ruled India, 1899–1901; a sketch by Lord Curzon." *Modern Review* 102 (August 1957): 114–19.
Curzon's opinion of his fellow administrators based on his private correspondence.

329. Abraham, F. "Was Lord Curzon's Indian policy a success?" *The Imperial and Asiatic Quarterly Review* 27 (1909).
Review of successes and failures of Curzon's viceroyalty.

330. Addy, Premen. "Imperial prophet or scaremonger?: Curzon's Tibetan policy reconsidered." *Asian Affairs* 14:1 (February 1983): 54–67.
Reviews Curzon's Tibetan policy in the light of criticism that it was "Russophobe, unrealistic, and overtly imperialistic." Subordination of Tibet to British control was not justified by any real threat to its autonomy from Russia or China nor was there a potential market for British goods.

331. "Anglo-Indian." "Lord Curzon in India, 1899–1905." *Monthly Review* 22 (March 1906): 73–89.
Favourable review of Curzon's term in India.

332. "Anglo-Indian" [Sir W. Lawrence]. "Lord Curzon's services to India." *North American Review* 176 (January 1903): 68–79.
Praise for Curzon's achievements from his former private secretary.

333. "An Onlooker." "Lord Curzon: an impression and a forecast." *Fortnightly Review* 70 (new series) 76 (old series) (October 1901): 700–8.
Defense of Curzon's work in India against "Clubland" critics at home stressing his reforms in education, famine relief, preservation of ancient monuments, etc.

334.   Arora, A.C. "Lord Curzon and political agency for the Phulkian States." *Ninth Punjab History Conference (Patiala): Proceedings* (1975): 195–204.
Study of Curzon's policies toward the Phulkian states.

335.   Arthur, Sir George. "Lord Curzon and Lord Kitchener." *Frontsoldat erzahlt* 84 (August 1905): 244–53.
On the Curzon-Kitchener controversy over "dual control" of the Indian Army.

336.   Arundel, A.T. "Decentralisation of government in India." *The Nineteenth Century and After* 65 (May 1909): 810–25, 66 (July 1909): 143–57.
Discusses Curzon's administrative reforms in this sphere and the recommendations of the Royal Commission of 1907.

337.   Ballard, C.R. *Kitchener*. London: Faber and Faber, 1930. 380.
Includes even-handed treatment of the "dual control" controversy showing how an official disagreement descended into a personality clash.

338.   Bandyopadhay, Premansukumar. "British famine and agricultural policies in India, with special reference to the administration of Lord George Hamilton, 1895–1903." Ph.D., London University 1969. 407.
India was hit by famines during 1896–97 and 1899–1900, the second of which was dealt with by Curzon. British government policy was dictated by a concern for economizing on relief expenditure. Hamilton was "illiberal" and prevented Curzon seeking further relief funds because of the wars in South Africa and China. An existing famine contingency fund had been misappropriated by earlier viceroys but the India Office would not allow Curzon to reclaim it. Curzon was genuinely concerned over the plight of India's rural poor but was hampered by "official restraints."

339.   Bardoux, J. "La question thibetaine et l'opinion britannique." *Revue Politique et Litteraire* 2 (July–December 1904): 388–93.
Reviews British attempts to establish relations with Tibet, Russian activity there, and the actions of Curzon as a background to the Younghusband expedition.

340.   Bence-Jones, Mark. *The viceroys of India*. London: Constable, 1982. 343.
Overview of the careers of every viceroy from Canning to Mountbatten with a chapter on Curzon's Indian career derived from secondary sources. The author concludes: "Curzon's achievement lay in the mechanics of administration rather than in the minds of men."

341.   Berard, V. "Lord Curzon et le Tibet." *Revue de Paris* 11 (January–February 1904): 881–94 and (March–April 1904): 197–224.
Detailed account of Curzon's relations with Tibet, emphasizing the influence of Ular's writings (see nos. 436–37 below) on Curzon in connection with Russian interest in Tibet.

342. Bhatia, L.M. "Curzon: a friend of India." *Indo-British Review* 11:2 (1985): 38–45.

Surveys Curzon's efforts to improve efficiency in the government of India.

343. ———. "The Kitchener quarrel." *Journal of Indian History* 56:3 (December 1978): 595–601.

Short account of the Kitchener-Curzon dispute over Indian military administration. Curzon was without doubt "wickedly treated" and his apprehensions about the future efficiency of the Indian Army completely vindicated by later events.

344. Bhattacharya, Sukumar. "Lord Curzon and Simla." *Bengal Past and Present* 87:2 (July–December 1968): 150–56.

Describes the development of Curzon's views on Simla from his early impressions of the attractiveness of its English climate to his feelings in 1903 about its monotony and dullness. Also included is his account of an earthquake there and the death and destruction wrought by it.

345. ———. "Lord Curzon and the Indian princes, 1899–1901." *Indian Historical Records Commission Proceedings* 33 (1958): 44–51.

Prints correspondence between Curzon and various Indian princes.

346. ———. "Lord Curzon's impressions of the Indian administration, 1898–1901." *Indian Historical Records Commission Proceedings* (Mysore) 31:2 (January 1955): 50–60.

Publishes selected extracts from Curzon's correspondence with Lord George Hamilton (among the Curzon papers in the India Office Library and Records) in which he comments frankly and confidentially on the abilities of fellow officials and military commanders in India.

347. Bhutani, V.C. "Curzon's educational reform in India." *Journal of Indian History* 51 (1973): 65–92.

Ascribes a political motivation to the various education conferences and commissions set up by Curzon, but accepts that genuine progress was made in the development of Indian education.

348. ———. "Some aspects of the administration of Lord Curzon." *Bengal Past and Present* 85:2 (July–December 1966): 159–82.

Reviews the positive aspects of Curzon's work as viceroy—his land administration, increased investment in Indian railways, monetary policy giving the rupee a gold value on the world market, legislation to encourage trade and industry and reorganization of the judiciary—but also recognizes the legacy of middle class resentment and eventual extremism that his failure to take account of Indian nationalism stimulated.

349. ———. "The administration of Lord Curzon's socio-economic policies." *Quarterly Review of Historical Studies* 8 (1968–69): 193–94.

Summarizes his Delhi University thesis which reviewed land revenue administration in late-Victorian India, the indebtedness of the agricultural classes, and Curzon's attempts to grapple with the problems. A supplementary chapter also looks at Curzon's education policies.

350. Brereton, J.M. "Mission to Tibet." *Blackwood's Magazine* 321 (1939): 433–47.
Examines Curzon's Tibetan policy 1898–1904.

351. Brodrick, William St. John Fremantle, Earl of Midleton. *Records and reactions 1856–1939*. London: John Murray, 1939. 318.
Brodrick came to the India Office in October 1903 with "serious misgivings" as Curzon had already become "increasingly trying to his friends" in the government (p. 186). Brodrick is concerned that the truth be known about the events leading up to Curzon's resignation, and as a close friend of long standing is revealing on Curzon's personality. Even before the Kitchener dispute the Cabinet had decided on Curzon's removal as his continuance in India in 1905 "was a danger to the Empire" (p. 188). The improvement in relations with Russia and the state of readiness of the Indian Army in 1914 alone justified the decision to accept Curzon's resignation.

352. ———. *Relations of Lord Curzon with the British government, 1902–5*. India Office, 1926.
His account of events leading up to Curzon's resignation, published as a State Paper.

353. Butt, Hamida I. "Development of education in India under Lord Curzon, 1899–1905." M. Phil., University of London, 1968.
Unpublished thesis.

354. Butt, Ikram A. "Lord Curzon and the Indian states, 1899–1905." Ph.D., University of London, 1964.
Analyzes Curzon's policies toward the princely states of India, including specific problems such as the education of princes in modern ways of government, their employment in the I.C.S. and Army, and moves towards centralization of political control. Issues receiving detailed treatment include the Delhi Durbar and the necessary deposing of some princes. Curzon saw the princes as the natural leaders of their people and wanted to educate them to their role in the hope that they would be a counterpoise to the nationalist movement.

355. "Calcutta." Article in *Contemporary Review* 78 (October 1900): 606.
Reply to article by "Civilis" below and defending Curzon's punishment of British troops in Burma.

356. Carey, Mussenden. "The decay of British rule in India: Lord Curzon's task of reform." *United Service Magazine* 144 (September 1901): 603.
Assesses the task facing Curzon if he is to make up for years of stagnation in Indian government.

357. "Civilis." "A progressive viceroy." *Contemporary Review* 78 (August 1900): 281.

Attacks what he feels was the excessiveness of Curzon's line in punishing British troops for misdemeanors in Burma in 1899.

358. Cohen, Stephen P. "Issue, role and personality: the Kitchener-Curzon dispute." *Comparative Studies in Society and History* 10:3 (April 1968): 337–55.

Concludes that there was no single cause of the disagreement between Curzon and Kitchener. Personal involvement, the issue at stake, and their respective roles all played their part in giving the dispute an "extraordinary bitterness."

359. Cotes, Mrs. E.C. "With Lord Curzon in Burma." *National Review* 39 (March 1902): 122–32.

Account of Curzon's recent visit to Burma where he impressed the Burmese not least by his decision to travel there so early in his viceroyalty.

360. Cullen, Major-General Sir E. "Lord Curzon, Lord Kitchener and Mr. Brodrick." *Blackwood's Magazine* 178 (September 1905): 427–44.

Detailed refutation of Kitchener's attacks on the "dual system" of Indian military administration and support for Curzon's stand against Brodrick and Kitchener on this issue.

361. Cotton, Henry. *India and home memories.* London: T.F. Unwin, 1911.

Deals with his leadership of the campaign against Curzon's Tibetan expedition, the justification for which he felt to be a "hollow pretence." British action, he claims, precipitated subsequent Chinese activity in the area.

362. Dalal, J.A.F. "Curzon in India." *Journal of the United Services Institution of India* 110 (459) (1980): 66–72.

Supposedly a review of Dilks's *Curzon in India* (no. 368a below), but mainly a factual summary of Curzon's administration.

363. Das, G.N. "Lord Curzon's concern for the past: an Indian tribute." *Asian Review* 58 (April 1962): 111–15.

Praise for Curzon's achievement in rescuing and restoring Indian historical monuments.

364. Das, M.N. "Curzon's successors and the partition of Bengal: a conflict in conscience." *Journal of Indian History* 39 (December 1961): 393–400.

How Morley and Minto attempted to cope with the problems of a partitioned Bengal bequeathed to them by Curzon.

365. ———. "Lord Curzon and the problems of European racialism in India." *Journal of Indian History* 39 (April 1961): 163–68.

For all the criticism of Curzon's failure to take account of Indian feeling he did at least deal firmly with racialism against Indians even though it resulted in his unpopularity in the British community.

366.   Davies, C. Collin. "Lord Curzon's frontier policy and the formation of the North-West Frontier Province, 1901." *Army Quarterly* 13 (1927): 261–73.

Curzon's frontier policy was not adventurous but sound, and was based on "withdrawal and concentration" leaving tribal troops recruited by the British to man isolated outposts. British troops were concentrated behind the frontier and communications with them improved. This policy and the creation of a North-West Frontier province helped secure a long period of tranquility on the frontier.

367.   ———. *The problem of the North West Frontier*. Cambridge: Cambridge University Press, 1932. 220.

Devotes a chapter to Curzon's imperial philosophy and frontier policy expanding on the article above.

368.   Dighe, V.G. "Lord Curzon and the national movement." *Journal of the Asiatic Society of Bombay* 39–40 (1964–65): 125–42.

Curzon's viceroyalty marked a watershed in the history of the Indian freedom movement. His régime put an end to any hope of peaceful development of Indian self-government. Curzon's highest ideal was efficiency of administration. He did not believe in the principle of liberty.

368a.   Dilks, David. *Curzon in India. Volume 1 Achievement. Volume 2 Frustration*. London: Rupert Hart-Davis, 1969–70. 603.

This study of Curzon's viceroyalty does not attempt a comprehensive record of his Indian career but is "episodic and selective" concentrating on issues that have interested the author. Thus there are sections on Curzon's policies toward Persia and Afghanistan, his relations with the India Office and Indian Army, and the great Durbar. The last is seen as the climax of his viceroyalty. Curzon himself appears as a talented, restless, and sensitive perfectionist. The second volume of the study develops several of the themes introduced earlier—his passion for administrative reform, a defense strategy for India based on a ring of buffer states, and the central role of India in the British Empire. To these are added "the ingredients of the final tragedy"—estrangement from the Cabinet, death of his first wife, and the breakdown in relations with Kitchener. The events surrounding his resignation are looked at in particular detail, as requested by Curzon at the end of his life, and a concluding chapter assesses the successes and failures of his viceroyalty.

369.   Dillon, E.J. "The mission to Tibet." *Contemporary Review* 85 (1904): 123–46.

Describes foreign press reaction to the British expedition to Tibet and attacks Curzon's policy.

370.   Dodwell, H.H. *Cambridge History of India. Vol. 6. Indian empire, 1858–1918*. London: Chand and Co., 1964. 759.

Factual account of Curzon's viceroyalty and administrative reforms.

371. Dutt, R.C., et al. *Land problems in India. . . .* Madras: 1903. 190.

Riposte by a former Indian civil servant to Curzon's Resolution of 1902 which set out and justified the principles of the British system of land assessment in India.

372. Edwardes, Michael. *High noon of Empire. India under Curzon.* London: Eyre and Spottiswoode, 1965. 266.

Sets out to explore the "nature of British rule in India" at the height of the raj for which a study of Curzon's viceroyalty offers a convenient medium. Aimed at a popular, rather than a specialist, readership, the book is based largely on secondary sources, e.g., it includes chapters entitled "Land of enchantment" and "The lion uncaged" (on Kitchener's dispute with Curzon). It benefits from Edwardes's wide knowledge of the history of British India and ability to place events in this period in a more general context. The main domestic and foreign issues of Curzon's viceroyalty are covered, and the concluding chapters look at the years after his departure in an assessment of his impact on Indian affairs.

373. ———. "The viceroyalty of Lord Curzon." *History Today* 12 (1962): 833–44.

Despite his imperialism and refusal to make concessions to Indian self-government Curzon's viceroyalty led "not to a restatement of power but to a failure of strength and purpose." He alienated the middle class and drove them into the arms of the more militant nationalist movement.

374. Fleming, Robert P. *Bayonets to Lhasa. The first full account of the British invasion of Tibet in 1904.* London: Rupert Hart Davis, 1961. 319.

Mainly an account of Younghusband's role in the mission but there is also much on Curzon's frontier policy, his dealings with Tibet, and his relations with Younghusband, and with Brodrick in London. On the background to the expedition: "It was his [Curzon's] mind that conceived the expedition to Tibet, his statecraft that overcame the obstacles to its launching; and many of the handicaps it carried had their origins in the prejudice which this brilliant, difficult man seldom failed to arouse against his policies and against himself" (p. 13). Fleming concludes that the most obvious result of the mission was "to lay Tibet open to a reassertion of Chinese authority" (p. 298)—the very thing it set out to prevent.

375. Fraser, Lovat G. *India under Curzon & after.* London: Heinemann, 1911. 496.

By the editor of the *Times of India* during Curzon's viceroyalty. The approach is not biographical, but is a "sketch of a period in which Lord Curzon was the central figure" (p. vi). This very personal, and at the time influential, view identifies education as the greatest source of conflict for Curzon. The outrage over Curzon's plans to divide Bengal is seen as having been grossly exaggerated for political purposes. Curzon's weaknesses are seen as his inability to distinguish between the trivial and the important, and his inability to accept criticism.

376. Fuller, Sir J.B. *Some personal experiences*. London: John Murray, 1930. 304.

Reminiscences of an I.C.S. official of some thirty years of Indian experience from c.1878, including service in the revenue department under Curzon at Calcutta and Simla. With the exception of the Delhi Durbar Curzon's viceroyalty was one of great achievement and his willingness to court the hostility of Anglo-Indian society over matters of principle is admired.

377. Gates, Rosalie P. The Tibetan policy of George Nathaniel Curzon viceroy of India, January 1899–April 1904, December 1904–November 1905. Ph.D., Duke University, 1965.

Unpublished thesis.

378. Ghosh, Suresh Chandra. *Indian nationalism: a case study for the first university reform by the British raj*. Ghaziabad: Vikas, 1985. 195.

Includes material on Curzon's role in the development of higher education in India.

379. Gilbert, Martin. "Famine in India: Sir Antony Macdonnell and a policy revolution in 1902." In Donovan Williams and E. Daniel Potts. *Essays in Indian history in honour of C. Collin Davies*. London: Asia Publishing House, 1973. 152–71.

How Curzon found support from Macdonnell for liberalizing British land settlement policies to help Indian peasants cope with famine.

380. Godley, Arthur, Baron Kilbracken. *Reminiscences of Lord Kilbracken*. London: Macmillan, 1931. 260.

View of Curzon's viceroyalty from the permanant secretary at the India Office. Curzon had great abilities and promised much during his short period as under-secretary at the India Office. However, he lacked the necessary tact for a good working relationship with London and turned the "dual control" episode into a personal affair. Brodrick is seen as an entirely competent Indian secretary who wisely stood his ground against Curzon and refused to allow him to take advantage of their past friendship.

381. Gopal, S. "Lord Curzon and the Indian nationalism." In S. N. Mukherjee (editor). *The movement for national freedom in India*. St. Antony's Papers, No. 18. Oxford: Oxford University Press, 1966. 114.

The beneficial effects of his rule in India led Curzon to underestimate the importance of nationalism in India which was fueled by the partition of Bengal.

382. Greenhurst, Frederick Adolph II. "The Tibetan frontier dispute from Curzon to the colonial conference." Ph.D., Syracuse University, 1972.

383. Grenard, F. "L'Angleterre et la Russe au Tibet." *Asie Française* 7 (1907): 375–83.

Examines Curzon's disagreement with the British government at home over his foreign policy, and other aspects of international relations with Tibet.

384. Grenville, John Ashley Soames. *Lord Salisbury and foreign policy: the close of the nineteenth century.* London: Athlone Press, 1964. 451.

Includes little on Curzon's service as under-secretary at the Foreign Office under Salisbury, but a section is devoted to Curzon's policy toward Persia as viceroy and his criticism of Salisbury's unwillingness to adopt a more forward policy in securing British influence in Persia. Quotes Curzon's exasperation at Salisbury's style of leadership: "There was no settled principles of policy in relation to any part of the world; and everyone from the exalted head down to the humblest clerk, sits there uneasily, waiting to see what will turn up next" (p. 297).

385. Hamilton, Angus. "Indo-Afghan relations under Lord Curzon." *Fortnightly Review* 86 (December 1906): 984–1000.

Account of relations between Russia and British India and Afghanistan under the Amir and his son, Habib Ullah Khan.

386. Hamilton, Lord George. *Parliamentary reminiscences and reflections.* London: John Murray, 2 vols., 1917, 1922. 684.

Volume two covers the period of Hamilton's Indian secretaryship. He has little to say of his own dealings with Curzon, but on the later question of "dual control" he makes the point that such a system had just been introduced to British army administration at home and that disasters during the Great War vindicated Curzon's stand in support of its continuance in the Indian Army.

387. Harischandra Anandarao Talcherkar. *Lord Curzon in Indian caricature: being a collection of cartoons . . . selected . . . and arranged with an elucidatory narrative by Harischandra A. Talcherkar.* Bombay: Babajee Sakharam, 1903. 52.

Compilation of cartoons by Indian artists, mainly from *Hindi-Punch*, the leading Anglo-Indian vernacular comic journal, caricaturing Curzon dealing with many of the important issues of his viceroyalty; with an explanatory narrative.

388. Harnetty, Peter. "Nationalism and imperialism in India (The viceroyalty of Lord Curzon, 1899–1905)." *Journal of Indian History* 41 (August 1963): 391–403.

Curzon's refusal to make concessions to Indian self-government made the leaders of the Congress turn from constitutional agitation to passive resistance, boycott, and the "swadeshi" movements. Curzon left behind him an unhappy legacy of discontent which led to terrorism and to British repression.

389. "Indian." "The Indian viceroy's tour." *Universal Magazine* 2 (March 1901): 468.

Illustrated account of Curzon's eight-week tour of India undertaken in the autumn of 1900.

390. Johnson, Paul. "Curzon's clash with the lordly Lancers." *Sunday Times Magazine* 30 April 1972, p. 25.

Account of Curzon's measures against the regiment, some of whose officers were involved in an assault on an Indian woman. Curzon's insistence on punishing the whole regiment lost him much popularity with Anglo-Indian society.

391. Joubert, J. "La demission de Lord Curzon." *Revue française de l'étranger et des colonies* 30 (1905): 579–89.

Deals with Curzon's career, his resignation, and his fears of Russian designs on Britain's empire in the East which led him into actions such as the invasion of Tibet.

392. Kaminsky, Arnold P. *The India Office, 1880–1910.* London: Mansell, 1986. 294.

Detailed study of the internal workings of the India Office during the permanent under-secretaryship of Sir Arthur Godley, 1st Lord Kilbracken. Curzon's relations with Godley, Lord George Hamilton, St. John Brodrick, Kitchener, the Council of India, and the Cabinet are all explored, with much incidental detail on Curzon's views on individuals and policies.

393. Kennion, R.L. "A country postman." *Blackwood's Magazine* 225 (1929): 83–95.

Account of his mission to deliver a letter from Curzon to the Garpon of Gartok in western Tibet for forwarding to the Dalai Llama.

394. Keswani, Dhan. "Story of the Taj lamp as gleaned through Curzon correspondence." *Indo-Asian Culture* 18:1 (January 1969): 9–17.

Story of Curzon's restoration of the Taj Mahal and his acquisition of a replacement for the original lamp in the upper mausoleum.

395. Khalfin, Naftula Aronovich. "Lord Kerson—ideolog i politik Britanskogo imperializma." [Lord Curzon: an idealogist and practitioner of British imperialism.] *Novaia i Noveishaia Istoriia* [USSR] 1 (1983): 120–40.

Concentrates on Curzon's influence on British imperialist policy, especially on the North-West Frontier; claims his ideas are still alive and kindle fires in present-day imperialists. Sources used include papers from the State Archives of Uzbek Soviet Socialist Republic.

396. Khare, Prakash. "What Naldera was to Curzon." *Times of India Magazine* 8 (30 December 1979): 5–8.

397. King, Peter. *The viceroy's fall. How Kitchener destroyed Curzon.* London: Sidgwick and Jackson, 1986. 310.

Existing works do not fully explain the motivations of the principal characters involved in the "dual control" dispute. The present study looks at why Curzon stubbornly engineered his own downfall, why Lord Salisbury and his family connection turned against him, and why Kitchener and later Brodrick "falsified" the facts to deny Curzon any credit for his contribution to Indian defense. "Naked ambition" to replace Curzon as viceroy contributed to Kitchener's motivation.

398.   Kohli, Manorama. "Curzon and his Tibet policy." *Quarterly Review of Historical Studies* 20:2–3 (1980–81): 36–46.

Opportunites for British trade clearly take second place to Anglo-Russian rivalry in explaining Curzon's Tibetan policy.

399.   Kumar, Ram Nandan. "A reappraisal of Lord Curzon's policy towards Afghanistan, Persia and the Persian Gulf region, 1899–1905." *Journal of Indian History* 56:3 (December 1978): 541–51.

Plays down the strategic reasons for Curzon's emphasis on the security of British India. This masked the "selfish designs of imperialists" like Curzon to perpetuate a British empire in India for its own sake, Curzon himself desiring to become a sort of "Great Mogul."

400.   Kumar, Ravindar. "Curzon and the Anglo-Russian negotiations over Persia, 1889–1901." *Proceedings of the Indian Historical Records Commission (Chandigarh)* 35:2 (February 1961).

Provides an able exposition of Curzon's Persian policy and his defeat of alternative proposals for appeasing Russia by offering concessions in Persia.

401.   ———. *India and the Persian Gulf region 1858–1907. A study in British imperial policy.* London: Asia Publishing House, 1965. 259.

Studies Curzon's relations with France over Oman, with Germany over Kuwait, and with Russia over Persia—all examples of his absolute conviction that Britain must be supreme in the Gulf and make no concessions to other Powers.

402.   Lawrence, Sir Walter Roper. *The India we served.* London: Cassell and Co., 1928. 318.

Important memoir of Curzon's viceroyalty by his friend and private secretary which looks at his strengths and weaknesses. Curzon's Victoria Memorial Hall scheme and his clash with Kitchener receive special treatment.

403.   Lipsett, H. Caldwell. "Lord Curzon in India." *Empire Review* 4 (December 1902): 479–85.

Review of the first four years of Curzon's term in India which is pronounced a success as a result of his reforming zeal. "He has impressed the native imagination by the strength of his personality . . . but still more by his untiring labours on behalf of the people of India."

404.   ———. *Lord Curzon in India 1898–1903. With an appendix containing Lord Curzon's speech justifying the Delhi Durbar.* London: R.A. Everett and Co., 1903. 143.

Fuller version of no. 403 above using extensive extracts from Curzon's speeches and writings to justify Curzon's policies at home and abroad. On the North-West frontier Curzon had supported "the dignity of empire" and had shown "firmness and enterprise" (p. 44). In domestic affairs, such as his famine administration, Curzon had silenced "those critics who maintain that native rule would be better than British rule" (p. 97). Curzon had proved himself the "best viceroy since Lord Lawrence" (p. 116).

405.   Lydgate, J.E. "Curzon, Kitchener and the problems of Indian army administration, 1899–1909." Ph. D., London University, 1965.
Unpublished thesis.

406.   Macdonald, J.M. "Lord Curzon." *Calcutta Review* 122 (October 1905): 531–52.
Laudatory review of Curzon's viceroyalty.

407.   McLane, J.R. "The decision to partition Bengal." *Indian Economic and Social History Review* 2 (July 1965): 221–37.
Explores the reasoning behind Curzon's decision to partition Bengal.

408.   ———. "The development of Nationalist ideas and tactics and the policies of the government of India 1897–1905." Ph.D., London University, 1961. 476.
Discusses the organization, ideas, and methods of Indian nationalism 1897–1905, the response of Elgin and Curzon as viceroys, and the latter's failure to recognize the strength of the movement.

409.   MacMunn, Sir George Fletcher. "The Kitchener-Curzon controversy and its results." *National Review* 91 (1928): 852–65.
Disputes Lord Ronaldshay's suggestion that the shortcomings of the Indian Army in the first part of the War were attributable to Kitchener's abolition of the "dual system" of military administration.

410.   Maconochie, Sir Evan. *Life in the Indian Civil Service*. London: Chapman and Hall, 1926. 269.
Important as the memoir of an Indian civil servant of long experience who welcomed Curzon's reforms and energy. Curzon is seen as the greatest viceroy of the time. As a result of his work "the house had been swept and garnished, the efficiency of its service improved and men . . . set to think who never thought before" (p. 122). Curzon did make mistakes, however, the most important of which was the partition of Bengal.

411.   Magnus, Philip. *Kitchener: portrait of an imperialist*. London: John Murray, 1958. 410.
In a chapter devoted to the troubles with Curzon Magnus concludes that Kitchener was right to abolish a military system which had become "obsolete and on the point of breaking down" (p. 226), but arrangements that replaced it gave the commander-in-chief too much work and in this way contributed to the Indian Army's poor showing in the Mesopotamian campaign.

412.   Malleson, Sir Wilfred. "Curzon and Kitchener; some personal reminiscences." *Fortnightly Review* 130 (old series) 124 (new series) (August 1928): 145–56.

Points out that the two men agreed on a number of areas of policy, such as their joint fears of the Russian threat to India. In hindsight Curzon's warnings that Kitchener's proposals for ending the "dual system" would lead to military dictatorship have been shown to be "claptrap" and any failures during the war were not as a result of this.

413. Martin, P. "Figures Indiennes disparues: Lord Curzon." *Asie Française* 25 (1925).
Review of Curzon's life and policies as viceroy and foreign secretary from a French point of view.

414. Mathur, D.B. "Lord Curzon and the politico-surgery of Bengal (October 16, 1905–December 12, 1911): a review." *Modern Review* 114 (October 1963): 270–82.
Analysis of Curzon's plans for the partition of Bengal.

415. Mehra, Parshotam L. "Kazi U-gyen and Lord Curzon's letter of 1901: a footnote." *Journal of Asian Studies* 26 (1967): 775–76.
Defends conduct of the Tibetan bearer of Curzon's dispatch to the Dalai Lama which was suspected never to have been delivered. No reply was received by the Indian government so precipitating the Younghusband expedition. The Dalai Lama had in fact refused to accept the letter and would only receive epistles from foreign governments through the agency of the Chinese.

416. ———. "Kazi U-gyen: a paid Tibetan spy?" *Journal of the Royal Central Asian Society* 51 (July–October 1964): 301–5.
As in his other article above, Mehra sets out to clear the name of Kazi U-gyen who was commonly believed to have failed to carry out his mission to the Dalai Lama with which he had been entrusted by Curzon.

417. ———. "Lord Curzon's despatch of January 8, 1903: its impact on his Tibetan policy." *Proceedings of the Indian History Congress* 21 (1958): 536–42.
Analyzes the background to the dispatch and its contents.

418. ———. "Tibet and Russian intrigue." *Journal of the Royal Central Asian Society* 45 (1958): 28–42.
Examines the nature of the threat supposedly offered by Russia to India and the nature of Russian activity in Tibet. Concludes that Curzon fell into a trap.

419. Mempes, Dorothy. *The Durbar.* 1903.
Eyewitness account of the great Durbar of 1903. Illustrations by Mortimer Mempes.

420. Milward, M.. "Nepal: the land that leads to paradise." *Asiatic Review* 35 (1939): 243–60.
An account of the role played by Sir Louis Dane, foreign secretary to the government of India, in persuading Curzon to meet Maharaja Chandra Shamsher

of Nepal in 1903 so improving Anglo-Nepalese relations before the Younghusband expedition to Tibet.

421. O'Donnell, Charles James (pseudonym). *The failure of Lord Curzon. A study in "Imperialism". An open letter to the Earl of Rosebery.* London: T. Fisher Unwin, 1903 (3rd. edition). 106.

Condemnation of Curzon's viceroyalty by an Indian administrator of 28 year's Indian experience. "Excepting the Durbar and its theatrical surroundings, which were an abomination to Anglo-Indians . . . Lord Curzon has done little. He has, indeed, appointed commissions on education . . . etc., but reform is still in the clouds. . . . There has in fact been much eloquence and imagination . . . but no achievements" (p. ix). Curzon is particularly criticized for his refusal to listen to officials with longer experience of India. An autocratic approach to government was right for India but not in the hands of a "pushful, ambitious young 'Imperialist'" with a reputation to make (p. xi). His domestic reforms had been ill-conceived, his foreign policies provocative. What India needed was "patient level-headedness" (p. 3).

422. "One of the people." *The partition of Bengal. An open letter to Lord Curzon.* Dacca: B. Chakravarty, [1904]. 18.

Sets out to refute Curzon's reasons for dividing Bengal on grounds of over-population. Bengalis shared a common religion and nationality and on these grounds should not be divided. Expresses the fears of East Bengalis about the "backwardness" of the Assam administration with which they were to be merged and about the extra competition for jobs, education, etc., from the population of Assam.

423. Ramaswamy, N.S. "Curzon and Indian monuments." *Indo-British Review* 1:2 (September–December 1968): 46–49.

An appreciation of Curzon's contribution to the rescue and restoration of ancient and historical buildings in India.

424. Ratcliffe, Samuel Kirkham. "Curzon in India. Fifty years after." *Contemporary Review* 1079 (November 1955): 299–302.

Short assessment of Curzon's Indian achievement 50 years after his resignation.

425. Richardson, H.E. "Russian intrigue in Tibet." *Journal of the Royal Central Asian Society* 46 (1959): 161–62.

Disputes the assertion of Mehra (no. 418 above) that, in his Tibetan policy, Curzon "fell into a Russian trap."

426. Rose, Kenneth. "Lord Curzon and the preservation of Indian monuments." *Apollo* 92 (August 1970): 144–45.

Illustrated account by one of Curzon's more recent biographers of his efforts to preserve and restore India's antiquities.

427. Rowji, Ramji Bin. "A petition on behalf of the rural poor of India to Lord Curzon." *East and West* 1 (January 1902): 265.
Appeal against Curzon's reforms in land assessment.

428. Roy, Krishna Chandra (Krishnachandra Raya). *Some desultory notes on Lord Curzon's work in India (January 1899–June 1901)*. Calcutta: S.K. Lahiri, 1902. 72.
Survey of first half of Curzon's viceroyalty by an Indian with long experience in the government education service; generally favorable to Curzon's domestic reforms, and recognizes Curzon's industry and knowledge. There is much quoting from Curzon's speeches and writings, and from the views of others on the viceroy's policies, but there is little direct criticism from the author himself; over education he contents himself with drawing attention to the principles that must be borne in mind in any reforms.

429. Sharma, A.P. "India's foreign problems and Lord Curzon (1899–1905)." *Journal of Historical Research* 12:1 (15 August 1969): 81–92.
Examines Curzon's policy in Afghanistan, Persia, and Tibet, and his relations with the India Office in London.

430. ———. "The Russian menace to India and Lord Curzon (1899–1905)." *Proceedings of the Indian History Congress* 31 (1969): 476–81.
Describes Curzon's attempts to counter Russian influences in Persia and Tibet, and his reactions to the Anglo-Russian Convention of 1907.

431. Sirdar Ali Khan, Syed. *Lord Curzon's administration of India: what he promised; what he performed*. Bombay: Times Press, 1905. 119.
Claims to speak for the majority of Indians in pronouncing Curzon's viceroyalty a brilliant success.

432. Sivasambhu Sarma. *Open letter to Lord Curzon*. 1905.
Printed translation of selected letters to the Indian newspaper *Bharat Mitra* condemning Curzon's viceroyalty for its "unnecessary and unsympathetic profusion of courtly splendour." However, his policies have galvanized Indian opposition. "The more strenuously Lord Curzon is exerting himself to bind them hand and foot, the more they are learning to move for the preservation of their lawful rights and privileges as subjects of the empire."

433. Srivastava, M.P. *British diplomacy in Asia: Persian Gulf, Soviet Central Asia, Tibet, China, India, and Burma*. New Delhi: Ess Ess Publications, 1978. 321.
Covers Curzon's policies toward the Persian Gulf states, China, Burma, etc., and imperial defense in S. Asia.

434. Steevens, G.W. "The installation of Lord Curzon as viceroy of India." *Scribner's Magazine* 25 (May 1899): 613.
Account of Curzon's assumption of office in India for the popular press.

435.   Strachey, Sir J. and Lt. General Sir R. Strachey. "Playing with fire: Mr. Brodrick and Lord Curzon." *National Review* 46 (1905): 593–620.

An attempt to give a reasoned account of the "dual control" controversy challenging Brodrick's claims about the benefits likely to arise from abolition of the existing military procedures in India and regretting Curzon's premature resignation.

436.   Ular, A. "L'Inde mysterieuse et la rivalité anglo-russe." *Revue* 54 (January–February 1905): 289–307.

Discusses Curzon's role in promoting Anglo-Russian rivalry on an Asia-wide scale.

437.   ———. "The Tibetan puzzle." *Contemporary Review* 85 (1904): 24–33.

Strongly supports Curzon's Tibetan policy.

438.   Wheeler, Stephen. *History of the Delhi Coronation Durbar.* London: 1904. 347.

Official account, with lavish illustrations, of the coronation Durbar of 1903.

439.   ———. "Lord Curzon in India." *Nineteenth Century and After* 49 (April 1901): 708–18.

Praises Curzon's achievements which have been overshadowed by the South African war; deals mainly with his frontier policy.

440.   Wilson, Sir Rowland K. Article written in reply to Rowji (no. 427 above). *East and West* 1 (July 1902): 895.

Refutation of the arguments against Curzon's land settlement reforms put by Rowji above.

441.   Woodruff, Philip. *The men who ruled India. The guardians.* London: Jonathan Cape, 1954. 385.

Account of the administrators of India from the Mutiny to 1909 which places Curzon in his Indian context.

442.   Wright, Sir Denis. "Curzon and Persia." *Geographical Journal* 153 (November 1987): 343–50.

443.   Younghusband, Sir Francis Edward. "Lord Curzon." *Nineteenth Century and After* 97 (1925): 621–33.

Describes Curzon's qualities and includes an account of his relations with him before and during the Tibetan expedition.

444.   Zaidi, Z.H. "The political motive in the partition of Bengal." *Journal of the Pakistan Historical Society* 12 (1964).

Studies the history of plans for the partition of Bengal which had first been mooted in the 1850s and concentrates on the evolution of Curzon's own ideas on the subject and their implementation. An assessment of their success or failure is left for others.

4. Political Office (1915–1925)

445. Anonymous. *Remarks on Lord Curzon's speech delivered on May 5th. 1921 in the House of Lords on the ratification of the Hungarian peace treaty of the Trianon. By a Transylvanian lady teacher.* Budapest, 1921. 32.

Disputes Curzon's assurances about the safety of Carpathia under Romanian rule and gives examples of Romanian abuses of civil liberties.

446. ———. "The change at the Foreign Office." *New Europe* 13:159 (30 October 1919).

One of a series of articles by radical politicians and academics calling for reform of the Foreign Office after the War. In this case Curzon's appointment as foreign secretary is welcomed as he is expected to have the strength of will to introduce "real reform" and to "bring the diplomatic service into touch with democratic currents at home and abroad."

447. Addison, Christopher, Viscount Addison. *A personal diary from four and a half years (June 1914–January 1919).* London: Hutchinson, 2 vols. 1934. 629.

Memoir of a fellow member of the War government in 1915 when he found Curzon "keen, straightforward and very clear-headed. In private dealings, he betrayed none of the stand-offishness and arrogance with which he is commonly credited . . ." (vol. 1, p. 85). Addison's recollections cover Curzon's periods in charge of shipping control and the Air Board.

448. Aitken, William Maxwell, Baron Beaverbrook. *Politicians and the war 1914–1916.* London: Thornton Butterworth, 1928. 240.

Memoir of politicians and events on the domestic front. It is revealing about Asquith's preference of Curzon to Law for the coalition government and for advice over the committee to look at national service in 1915. Beaverbrook thought Curzon no "political mediocrity" despite his unpopularity.

449. ———. *The decline and fall of Lloyd George.* London: 1963.

Describes the years 1921–22 and the divisions between Lloyd George and Curzon over foreign policy, the sale of honors, etc.

450. Andrew, Christopher. "Codebreakers and Foreign Offices: the French, British, and American experiences." In Christopher Andrew and David Dilks (editors). *The missing dimension: governments and intelligence communities in the twentieth century.* Macmillan, 1984. 33–54.

451. ———. *Secret service: the making of the British intelligence community.* London: Heinemann, 1985. 859.

Describes Curzon's opposition to the Anglo-Russian trade talks of 1920 and his naive public use of intelligence obtained through British deciphering of Russian codes.

452. Busch, Briton Cooper. *Britain, India and the Arabs, 1914–1921*. Berkeley: 1971. 522.

Studies the British war effort and concentrates on competition between government departments for control of policy in the Middle East.

453. ———. *Mudros to Lausanne: Britain's frontier in west Asia, 1918–1923*. Albany, 1976.

Study of British policy in the Middle East, concentrating on inter-departmental rivalry for control and between the India Office and the government of India.

454. "Christophe" [pseudonym]. *Les douze commandements de Lord Curzon pour le temps de guerre interpretés et illustrés par Christophe*. Paris: Librairs Armand Colin, 1915. 36.

Satirical version of Curzon's twelve precepts for "How a nation should behave in time of war" (see no. 262 above), illustrated with cartoons for each precept, e.g.: "Don't be unnerved by personal or family bereavements." Reaction of "Belgian" in cartoon: "When I think that out of those ruins shall come forth a new Europe it makes me forget that my house once stood there." Text in English, French, and Italian.

455. Close, David H. "The collapse of resistance to democracy: Conservatives, adult suffrage and second chamber reform." *Historical Journal* 20:4 (1977): 893–918.

Study of the role of Curzon and other leading Tories in formulating party policy on these issues.

456. Crozier, Andrew J. "The establishment of the mandates system, 1919–25: some problems created by the Paris Peace Conference." *Journal of Contemporary History* 14 (July 1979): 483–513.

Sees the mandate system as a compromise between the post-war idealism of British and American socialists and the desire of the Allies to retain their wartime conquests. Curzon resists French attempts to make the mandates more like colonies and his relations with the Americans and the French over the distribution of the mandates is also discussed.

457. Darwin, John G. *Britain, Egypt and the Middle East; imperial policy in the aftermath of war, 1918–1922*. New York: Macmillan, 1981. 333.

Studies Curzon's policies toward Egypt, Persia, Russia, and Turkey. Curzon's "indocentric" approach was based on the destruction of Turkey to ensure the safety of sea routes to India. However, his autocratic background did not make him inflexible. His "imperial system relied on techniques of political control which must vary from place to place."

458. ———. "The Chanak crisis and the British cabinet." *History* 65 (1980): 32–48.

Re-examines the crisis which has been seen by historians as symptomatic of various things. Curzon's policy marked a fundamental change in the British line toward Turkey: he was not concerned with defending her but ensuring that she was never again able to threaten British supremacy in the East, i.e., strip her of her European possessions and control of the Straits. Events overtook him but the whole Cabinet is shown to have been in general agreement with his policy. Curzon's motives for abandoning the coalition government of Lloyd George are put down in gossip to his fear of making a mistake and distancing himself from a policy he no longer had confidence in. Austen Chamberlain wrote: "I could see him in those last days lashing himself into fury in order to justify the defection which he contemplated . . . the fact is that he is a funker and a bad man to go tiger-shooting with." In fact there was much continuity of policy in the new government in which Curzon was foreign secretary.

459. Dockrill, Michael L. "The Foreign Office and the 'Proposed Institute of International Affairs.' " *International Affairs* 56:4 (1980): 665–72.
Describes the buildup to the establishment of the Institute (later the Royal Institute of International Affairs) in 1920 with details of Curzon's opposition to it on the grounds that F.O. staff who joined would be at liberty to discuss confidential policy matters with American members. This seemed to him "subversive of discipline and derogatory to the authority of the Secretary of State," prompting Lord Robert Cecil to respond: "I am sure that the conception of the Foreign Office, that it is the private property of the Secretary of State, is incompatible with any real confidence in it by the public." (Quoted pp. 670–71.)

460. Dockrill, Michael L. and J. Douglas Gould. *Peace without promise: Britain and the peace conferences, 1919–1923.* London: Batsford, 1981. 287.
Based on the private papers of Curzon, Hardinge, Balfour, etc., and on official Foreign Office and Cabinet records, Curzon's policy in the Middle East and the Balkans is explored. The study is particularly concerned with the "role and attitudes of top British policy-makers."

461. Egerton, George W. "Britain and the 'Great Betrayal': Anglo-American relations and the struggle for United States ratification of the Treaty of Versailles, 1919–1920." *Historical Journal* 21:4 (1978): 885–911.
Studies Anglo-American relations over the formation of the League of Nations, particularly the role played by Lord Grey, British ambassador in Washington. Curzon's difficult relations with Grey are explored, including Grey's determination to write his own instructions and to appease the Americans. Grey wanted the League to take second place to British policies in the Middle East. Curzon told Lloyd George that Grey was "too disposed to dictate a policy to your government than to carry out their views. . . ." Egerton contends that the failure to bring America into the League confirmed Curzon's prediction of American untruthfulness and allowed him to concentrate on the British imperial dimension.

462. Elcock, H.J. "Britain and the Russo-Polish frontier, 1919–1921." *Historical Journal* 12:1 (1969): 137–54.

Studies the principles behind British policy toward Poland with references to Curzon's role and the creation of the "Curzon Line" between Poland and Russia.

463. Fatemi, Nasrollah Saifpour. *Diplomatic history of Persia 1917–1923: Anglo-Russian power politics in Iran.* New York: Russell F. Moore Co., 1952. 331.

Detailed and lengthy account of Anglo-Persian relations from the Persian point of view, with much on Curzon's policies.

464. Fraser, Peter. "The Unionist debacle of 1911 and Balfour's retirement." *Journal of Modern History* 35 (1962): 354–65.

Touches on Curzon's role in the Tory party's attitude to constitutional reform in 1911 and in urging Balfour to accept the reality of the Liberal threat to create new peers; also Curzon's attitude to Balfour's decision to give up the Tory party leadership.

465. Goold, J. Douglas. "Lord Hardinge as ambassador to France, and the Anglo-French dilemma over Germany and the Near East." *Historical Journal* 21:4 (1978): 913–37.

Studies Hardinge's involvement as British representative in Paris in such questions as reparations, upper Silesia, a proposed Anglo-French pact, disarmament in Germany and allied policies in the Near East, showing how he and Curzon worked closely together. They were united in seeking a peaceful compromise with France over the outstanding issues of the time and in their opposition to Lloyd George's independent foreign policy making. Hardinge's views were sought frequently by Curzon during the Chanak crisis and it was to Hardinge that Curzon turned when Poincaré was at his most impassioned during negotiations.

466. Gregory, John Duncan. *On the edge of democracy: rambles and collections, 1902–1928.* London, 1929.

Recollections of a former assistant secretary at the Foreign Office under Curzon, including a vivid account of Curzon's manner toward, and relations with, his staff.

467. Hardinge, Charles, Baron Hardinge. *Old diplomacy: the reminiscences of Lord Hardinge of Penshurst.* London: John Murray, 1947. 288.

As a former viceroy himself, approached his under-secretaryship at the Foreign Office under Curzon with some trepidation, particularly as Curzon had been an implacable opponent of his Indian policies. However, Hardinge's memoir contains much on Curzon's reliance on him in the House of Lords when he went to France as ambassador in 1920 in a period of strained Anglo-French relations.

468. Harrison, Brian. *Separate spheres: the opposition to women's suffrage in Britain.* London: Croom Helm, 1978. 274.

Curzon's role in the National League for Opposing Women's Suffrage is fully explored with particular emphasis on his relations with other leaders of the movement (male and female), his contribution, with Lord Cromer, to the financial organization of the movement, and his flare for publicizing its objectives. His reasons for oppposing the vote for women are also dealt with and their link with his imperialistic viewpoint. "For the discharge of great responsibilities in the dependencies of the Empire . . . you want the qualities not of the feminine but of the masculine mind" (p. 75).

469. Hazlehurst, Cameron. *Politicians and the war.* London: Jonathan Cape, 1971.

Studies the role and attitude of Curzon and other politicians during the war.

470. Helmreich, Paul C. *From Paris to Sèvres: the partition of the Ottoman Empire at the Peace Conference of 1919–1920.* Columbus, Ohio: Ohio State University Press, 1974. 376.

Detailed study of this area of Allied post-war foreign policy and of Curzon's role in shaping the British standpoint.

471. Hinsley, F.H. *British foreign policy under Sir Edward Grey.* Cambridge: Cambridge University Press, 1977. 702.

Includes articles by many scholars on different aspects of policy, providing invaluable background to Curzon's term of office as foreign secretary.

472. Hooker, James R. "Lord Curzon and the 'Curzon line.' " *Journal of Modern History* 30 (1958): 137–38.

Based on secondary sources claims that Curzon did not devise this boundary between Russia and Poland; in a note to the Russian foreign commissar of 11 July 1920 Curzon in fact had referred to a line drawn between Russia and Poland in the previous year to which he felt the Russians might be persuaded to withdraw to enable peace talks with Poland.

473. Hopkins, M.F. "The politics of peacemaking: Lord Curzon, the prime minister and the cabinet and the making of peace with Turkey, January 1922– July 1923." M.A., Leeds University, 1986.

474. Jeffery, Keith. *The British Army and the crisis of empire, 1918–22.* Manchester: Manchester University Press, 1984. 200.

Shows how Curzon's policies for protecting India from the threat of Russian invasion by maintaining a "cordon sanitaire" of buffer states along India's frontiers was felt to be impracticable by Wilson and other military strategists.

475. ————. *The military correspondence of Field-Marshal Sir Henry Wilson, 1918–22.* London: Bodley Head, 1985. 438.

Includes Wilson's correspondence with Curzon in this period as well as letters from others throwing light on Curzon's foreign policy, toward Russia particularly.

476. Jenkins, Roy. *Mr. Balfour's poodle. An account of the struggle between the House of Lords and the government of Mr. Asquith.* London: Heinemann, 1954. 224.

Examines Curzon's motives during the constitutional crisis for changing from outright opposition to abstention.

477.   Jones, Thomas. *Whitehall diary*. Edited by Keith Middlemas. Volume 1. 1916–1925. London: Oxford University Press, 1969. 358.

Diary kept by the assistant secretary to the coalition Cabinet from 1916 with accounts of daily proceedings and Curzon's contributions, with many insights in later years into Curzon's dealings with his staff at the Foreign Office.

478.   Kent, Marian. ''Guarding the band wagon: Great Britain, Italy, and Middle Eastern oil, 1920–1923.'' In Edward Ingram (editor). *National and international politics in the Middle East. Essays in honour of Elie Kedourie*. London: Frank Cass, 1986. 146–63.

Studies the rival attempts of Curzon and the Italian government to get oil concessions in the Middle East.

479.   Larew, Karl G. ''Great Britain and the Greco-Turkish War, 1921–1922.'' *Historian* 35 (February 1973): 256–70.

Explores the position of Britain, and of Curzon in particular, in the lead up to the Chanak crisis.

480.   Lloyd George, David, Earl Lloyd George. *Memoirs of the peace conference*. New York: Howard Fertig, 1972 (2nd edition). 2 vols., 964.

Throws light on Curzon's advocacy of a trial for the Kaiser in 1918, his unwillingness to surrender Georgia to the Russians, his reservations about the feasibility of a Zionist settlement in Palestine, and his support for the creation of an Armenian state. Lloyd George finishes with a condemnation of the ''humiliating'' Treaty of Lausanne when Curzon abandoned the idea of an independent enlarged Armenia: ''an abject, cowardly and infamous surrender'' (p. 872).

481.   ———. *War memoirs of David Lloyd George*. London: Ivor Nicholson and Watson, 1936. 6 vols., 3531.

Includes many references to Curzon's membership of the War Cabinet, providing interesting background to his presidency of the Air Board and struggles with the Admiralty to establish the Board's autonomy.

482.   Louis, William Roger. *Great Britain and Germany's lost colonies 1914–1919*. Oxford: Clarendon Press, 1967. 165.

Useful analysis of Curzon's views on the need to deprive Germany of her African colonies at the peace settlement for the future security of the British Empire.

483.   Lytton, Victor A.G.R. Bulwer, Earl of Lytton. *Two voices in the St. Andrew's Hall, Glasgow. Refutation by Lord Lytton, suffragist, December 9th. 1912, of the arguments of Lord Curzon, anti-suffragist, November 1st. 1912*. Edinburgh: Conservative and Unionist Women's Franchise Association, 1913. 14.

Refutation of all Curzon's arguments against the vote for women, accusing him of displaying an "amazing ignorance . . . of women and of politics."

484. McEwen, J.M. (editor). *The Riddell diaries 1908–1923*. London: Athlone Press, 1986. 430.
Prints the full text of Riddell's diaries, much of which had been left out of the earlier edition (see no. 503 below). There are references to Curzon from 1915 covering his support for national service and elsewhere some early impressions of Curzon from Lloyd George: "He has travelled a lot; he knows about the countries of the world. He has read a lot. He is full of knowledge which none of us possess . . . he is not a good executant and has no tact but he is valuable. . . ." The diary also records, however, the later conflict between the two over foreign policy in the early twenties.

485. Macfie, A.L. "The Chanak affair (September–October 1922)." *Balkan Studies* 20:2 (1979): 309–41.
Discusses how Curzon managed to get the Turks to respect the neutrality of the Straits even after the Greeks had been driven back, and how an armistice was concluded. He succeeded thereby in safeguarding the allied position in the region in preparation for the Conference of Lausanne.

486. ———. "The Straits Question: the Conference of Lausanne (November 1922–July 1923)." *Middle Eastern Studies* 15:2 (1979): 211–38.
How Curzon managed to secure the "freedom of the Straits" for the Allies at Lausanne.

487. Marcovitch, Lazare. "Lord Curzon and the Pashitch: light on Jugoslavia, Turkey and Greece in 1922. A personal record by Lazare Marcovitch." *Journal of Central European Affairs* 13 (1953): 329–37.
As a member of Pashitch's Yugoslavian government Marcovitch accompanied him to the Paris Peace Conference. His account describes Curzon's attempt to involve the Yugoslavians in an independent scheme to deprive Turkey of control of the Straits and Pashitch's refusal to participate without French cooperation.

488. Marks, Sally. "Ménage à trois: the negotiations for an Anglo-French-Belgian alliance in 1922." *International History Review* 4:4 (November 1982): 524–52.
Discusses the role of Curzon and Lloyd George in negotiations with France and Belgium toward the conclusion of a treaty guaranteeing British help in the eventuality of another war. Curzon was concerned that any treaty should not be open-ended and should specify Germany as the potential aggressor to minimize chances of British involvement in another continental war.

489. Medlicott, William N. *British foreign policy since Versailles 1919–1963*. London: Methuen, 2nd. ed., 1968. 362.
Standard work which places Curzon's foreign secretaryship in the context of British twentieth-century foreign policy.

490.   Mitchell, John M. *Colonial statesmen and votes for women. Lord Curzon answered, etc.* London: Women's Freedom League, 1913. 8.

Publishes the results of questionnaires put to colonial representatives at the Imperial Conference of 1911 and attending the coronation of George V on their experience of women's suffrage which, the author claims, refute all Curzon's arguments against granting women the vote.

491.   Montgomery, A.E. "Lloyd George and the Greek Question, 1918– 1922." In A.J.P. Taylor (editor). *Lloyd George: twelve essays.* London: Hamish Hamilton, 1971. 257–84.

Reassessment of Lloyd George's part in the war between Greece and Turkey and the Chanak crisis based on British public records. Considerable doubt is thrown on Curzon's charges that Lloyd George was conducting a secret diplomacy with the Greeks.

492.   ———. "The making of the Treaty of Sèvres of 10 August 1920." *Historical Journal* 15 (1927): 775–87.

Study of Anglo-French negotiations over Turkey in the build-up to the Treaty, discussing the roles of Curzon and Lloyd George in drafting the Treaty. Curzon's part in supporting Lloyd George in policies he didn't always approve of so that the French might be kept in check is also brought out.

493.   Morgan, Kenneth O. *Consensus and disunity: the Lloyd George coalition government, 1918–1922.* Oxford: Clarendon Press, 1979. 436.

Argues that Curzon and Lloyd George were in agreement over most areas of foreign policy. "It was protocol that Curzon largely objected to, rather than the substance of Lloyd George's policies" (p. 114).

494.   Nassibian, Akaby. *Britain and the Armenian question, 1915–1923.* London: Croom Helm, 1984. 294.

Includes extensive material on Curzon and his policies in relation to Armenia.

495.   Nicolson, Harold George. "Curzon." *Foreign Affairs* 7:2 (1929): 221– 33.

Memoir of Curzon's career by his former colleague and biographer.

496.   ———. *Curzon: the last phase 1919–1925. A study in post-war diplomacy.* London: Constable and Co., 1934 (1st. edition). 416.

Study of Curzon's foreign secretaryship based on personal knowledge and Curzon's papers. Curzon's personality and background are taken account of in this assessment. They were contributory factors, along with his lack of political skill, in his overall failure as a politician. In foreign affairs he failed to halt the deterioration in Britain's place in the world. There are detailed chapters on such issues as Greco-Turkish relations, Persia, Egypt, and reparations. Curzon's relationship with Lloyd George is also explored and Nicolson doesn't necessarily agree that Lloyd George involved himself too much in foreign affairs. Some areas, such as Russia, were left entirely to Curzon. In all, a franker assessment than Nicolson's *D.N.B.* entry for Curzon (see no. 301 above).

497. ———. *Some people*. London: Folio Society edition, 1951. 180.

Series of essays about events and people experienced or encountered during Nicolson's life, including this amusing anecdote of his journey to the continent as a member of Curzon's Lausanne Conference party with special reference to the problems caused by Curzon's recently appointed valet.

498. Northedge, F.S. "The ideal civil servant? Lord Curzon's relationship with Lloyd George." *The Listener* (31 December 1959): 1149–51.

Explores the working relationship between Curzon and Lloyd George about which Curzon complained constantly but nevertheless continued to accept.

499. Olson, William J. "The genesis of the Anglo-Persian agreement of 1919." In Elie Kedourie and Sylvia Haim (editors). *Towards a modern Iran: studies in thought, politics and society*. London: Frank Cass, 1980.

Discusses Curzon's policy, in the face of Persian nationalism and American and French hostility, to make Persia a buffer state for the protection of India.

500. O'Malley, Sir Owen. *The phantom caravan*. London: John Murray, 1954. 262.

Memoir of a senior official in the Foreign Office during Curzon's period in charge in which he expresses the usual admiration for Curzon's industry, grasp of detail, "outsize intelligence and character" (p. 59) etc., but also describes his occasional "callousness" to colleagues, such as Sir Eyre Crowe, whom he disliked.

501. Pugh, Martin D. "Politicians and the women's vote, 1914–1918." *History* 49 (1974): 358–74.

Reassesses the importance of the War for the women's suffrage movement and concludes that the 1918 Representation of the People Act in fact only offered women what they had found unacceptable in 1912. Curzon's relations with the anti-suffragists is explored, particularly his unwillingness for use to be made of the League's assets. His speech against the measure in the Lords, followed by his unexpected exhortation to abstain, is blamed for its success in the Lords.

502. Ramsden, John (editor). *Real old Tory politics. The political diaries of Sir Robert Sanders, Lord Bayford, 1910–35*. London: Historians Press, 1984. 260.

Interesting as the political diary of an "old school" Tory who was many years a whip and eventually Minister of Agriculture. He kept a political diary from 1910 to 1929 which includes details of Curzon's role in the constitutional crisis of 1910–11 and his unwillingness to be party to a coalition between Liberals and Tories in 1918 as he regarded Lloyd George as a "dirty little rogue" (p. 102).

503.   Riddell, George A., Lord Riddell. *Lord Riddell's war diary 1914–1918*. London: Nicholson and Watson, 1933. 388.
Information about Curzon is largely covered in McEwen above (no. 484).

504.   ———. *Lord Riddell's intimate diary of the Peace Conference and after*. London: Gollancz, 1933. 435.
A fuller version of the diary has been edited by McEwen (see no. 484 above), but the present volume reproduces two particularly important conversations between Riddell and Curzon in 1920 when the latter reviews his childhood, relations with his father, early love of the East, and his viceroyalty; and in 1923 when he gives his opinion of Baldwin and Lloyd George and complains that he had always been misunderstood.

505.   Rowland, Peter. *Lloyd George*. London: Barrie and Jenkins, 1975. 872.
Competent biography of Lloyd George with much on his relationship with Curzon during the war and over foreign policy in the 1920s, including the Chanak crisis, the Anglo-Russian trade treaty, etc.

506.   Rush, Dorothy Boyd. "Lord Curzon and Kemalism; the old world and the new East." *Social Science* 55:2 (1980): 77–88.
Curzon hoped for enduring monuments and lasting treaties in the Middle East; what he did was to help orchestrate a relatively smooth transition from the old world to the new in that part of the world.

507.   Schofield, Stephen. "Aristocratic crumble—caused by a Canadian." *Dalhousie Review* 51:1 (1971): 31–37.
Claims that Bonar Law, "a Canadian from New Brunswick," refused to recommend Curzon as future premier as he had received an angry letter from him on a minor subject and felt that "he could not entrust the destiny of Britain to one who could become so influenced over such a trivial matter."

508.   Sharp, Alan J. "Britain and the Channel Tunnel 1919–1920." *Australian Journal of Politics and History* 25:2 (August 1979): 210–15.
Describes earlier schemes for a tunnel and discusses the attitudes of Curzon at the Foreign Office and other ministers when the question came up again after the War. There was much instinctive hostility to such a physical link with the continent which may have counted for more than the strategic counter-arguments. As Curzon said, "the teachings of history" were against.

509.   ———. "Lord Curzon and secret intelligence." In Christopher Andrew and Jeremy Noakes (editors). *Intelligence and international relations 1900–1945*. Exeter University, 1987. 103–26.

510.   ———. "Lord Curzon and the Foreign Office." In Roger Bullen (editor). *The Foreign Office 1782–1982*. Frederick (Maryland): University Publications of America Inc., 1984. 66–84.
The status of the Foreign Office suffered under Curzon, who was unable to

prevent Lloyd George involving other departments such as the War Office, Treasury, and the Prime Minister's own office in negotiations such as reparations and excluding the Foreign Office. There was a resulting lack of confidence in Curzon within the Foreign Office at his failure to curb Lloyd George's interference in foreign affairs and his predeliction for appointing outsiders to diplomatic posts.

511. ———. "Some relevant historians; the political intelligence department and the Foreign Office, 1918–1920." *Australian Journal of Politics and History* (forthcoming volume).

512. ———. The Foreign Office in eclipse, 1919–1922." *History* 61 (1976): 198–218.
Contributory factors toward the declining status of the Foreign Office in this period were the meddling in policy making of Lloyd George and Curzon's inability to cope with this. However, the main cause was Curzon's inability to control and weld together the numerous individuals and offices involved in formulating and administering British foreign policy.

513. Smith, Michael Llewellyn. *Ionian vision: Greece in Asia Minor, 1919–1922.* London: Allen Lane, 1973. 401.
Detailed and step-by-step account of the Greco-Turkish crisis in this period and of Curzon's involvement with Lloyd George, the French, and other allies.

514. Steiner, Zara and M.L. Dockrill. "The Foreign Office at the Paris Peace Conference in 1919." *International History Review* 2:1 (January 1980): 55–86.
Shows how Lloyd George and his immediate circle monopolized negotiations for the British and failed to keep the Foreign Office in London informed of progress. Even British officials in Paris were kept in the dark and were unable to answer inquiries from Curzon about the current line of British policy. Curzon's memoranda are quoted to illustrate his frustration with Lloyd George and with Balfour whose lassitude he blamed for the level of prime ministerial interference.

515. ———. "The Foreign Office reforms, 1919–1921." *Historical Journal* 17:1 (1974): 131–56.
Describes reforms of this period including reduction of the War period complement, attempts to unify the domestic and overseas branches of the service, and improvements in office practice. Great things were expected of Curzon in all three areas of reform. He did not go wholeheartedly for the idea of a unified service, however, and compromised so as to build up a pool of experienced London-based staff.

516. Sworakowski, W. *An error regarding Eastern Galicia in Curzon's note to the Soviet Government of July 11, 1920.* Privately printed in the United States, 1944. 26.
Documents the result of an editorial error in Curzon's "note" which placed

Eastern Galicia to the east of the "Curzon Line" and thereby allowing it to be claimed by Russia in 1944.

517.   Temperley, Harold W.V. (editor). *A history of the Peace Conference of Paris (1920–4).* London: Hodder and Stoughton, 1920–24. 6 vols., 3180.

Monumental and definitive in its detailed account of the Conference describing its organization and personnel, with volumes on issues such as reparations, central Europe, protection of minorities, the Near and Middle East, the League of nations, etc. Essential background to Curzon's foreign secreteryship.

518.   Ullman, Robert Henry. *Anglo-Soviet relations 1917–1921.* Oxford: Oxford University Press, 1961, 1968, 1972. 3 vols. 1257.

Studies Curzon's Russian policy and also suggests that the Foreign Office was often more sympathetic to Lloyd George's involvement in foreign affairs than its chief.

519.   Vansittart, Robert G, Baron Vansittart. *The mist procession. The autobiography of Lord Vansittart.* London: Hutchinson, 1958. 568.

Autobiography of a former diplomat and private secretary to Curzon 1920–24.

520.   Vincent, Edgar, Viscount d'Abernon. *An ambassador of peace: papers from the diary of Viscount D'Abernon (Berlin 1920–1926).* London: Hodder and Stoughton, 3 vols., 1929–30. 985.

Includes an appreciation of Curzon's diplomacy (vol. 1, pp. 48–52) putting his great qualities before his faults. The remaining volumes describe Curzon's dealings with Poincaré, and, later, an account of Curzon's handing over the Foreign Office when Ramsay Macdonald's government came in.

521.   Walder, David. *The Chanak affair.* London: Hutchinson, 1969. 380.

Includes extensive material on Curzon's involvement, particularly on his negotiations with Poincaré and on the conference at Lausanne.

522.   Ward, Sir Adolphus William and George Peabody Gooch (editors). *The Cambridge history of British foreign policy, 1783–1919.* Cambridge: Cambridge University Press, 1923. Vol. 3. 664.

Vol. 3 covers the period 1866–1919; little on the first year of Curzon's foreign secretaryship but some detail of his views on Persia, Tibet, and Afghanistan as viceroy, and his opposition to the entente with Russia in 1905–7.

523.   White, Stephen. *Britain and the Bolshevik revolution. A study in the politics of diplomacy, 1920–1924.* London: Macmillan, 1979. 317.

Includes much on Curzon and negotiations toward a trade agreement with Russia, on Curzon's hostility to Russia, and the influence of his Indo-centric view of the Empire on his attitude.

524.   Williamson, David G. "Great Britain and the Ruhr crisis, 1923–1924." *British Journal of International Studies* 3 (1977): 70–91.

525. Woods, Charles H. "Lord Curzon and Lausanne." *Fortnightly Review* 5 (March 1923): 491–502.

Discusses the international ramifications of the conference and credits Curzon with a great success for British diplomacy.

526. Woodward, E.L. and Rohan Butler, et al. (editors). *Documents on British foreign policy, 1919–1939.* London: HMSO, 1947–. First series, vols. 1–27.

Publishes documents relating to the peace treaties, Europe, the Near and Far East 1919–25 with much detail of Curzon's involvement in British foreign policy.

5. Other Public Offices and Interests

527. Goudie, A.S. "George Nathaniel Curzon: superior geographer." *Geographical Journal* 146:2 (July 1980): 203–9.

Curzon was not always admired inside the Royal Geographical Society for his manner, but he made great contributions to political geography and exploration, not only in his own right, but also in his encouragement of explorers such as Hedin, Stein, and Huntington. He transformed the RGS during his presidency and encouraged the admission of women fellows.

528. Morton, Catherine. *Bodiam Castle, Sussex.* National Trust, 1986 (1st. edition 1981).

Guidebook to the castle, covering its history and Curzon's role in its restoration.

529. National Trust. *Tattershall Castle, Lincolnshire.* National Trust, 1988.

Short history of the medieval castle which Curzon purchased in 1911 following an outcry over the sale of some of its architectural features; resulted in the Ancient Monuments Act of 1913.

530. Urquhart, F.–F. "Lord Curzon and Oxford reform." *Dublin Review* 145 (July–October 1909): 138–46.

Assessment of Curzon's proposals for reform of Oxford University which are seen as falling under two main heads: improving efficiency and opening the door to a wider range of students.

6. Members of Curzon's Family

531. Bryant, F. Russell. "Lady Curzon, the Marchioness from Decatur." *Alabama History Quarterly* 44:3–4 (1982): 213–60.

Biographical sketch of Grace Hinds (1878–1958) who, as Mrs. Duggan, became Curzon's second wife; covers her early life in Alabama, her marriages, and her emergence as one of London's premier society hostesses.

532. Chatterjee, Raj. "Mary—the American vicereine." *Hindustan Times Magazine* 22 August 1982. 1–8.

Journalistic account of Mary Curzon's years in India as vicereine.

533. Fowler, Marian. *Below the peacock fan: first ladies of the Raj*. London: Viking, 1987. 337.

Account of the Indian experience of Emily Eden, Charlotte Canning, Edith Lytton, and Mary Curzon based on their writings. The last three went to India as consorts of governors-general or viceroys. India had a profound effect on all of them but their reactions to their experience were conditioned by their own personalities, their relationship with their husbands (or brother in the case of Emily Eden), and by the momentous changes taking place in the sub-continent during Victoria's reign.

534. Moorehead, Caroline. "Lady Alexandra Metcalfe. Daughter of the Raj who is a jewel in the crown." *The Times* 15 October 1984. 11.

Article based on an interview with Curzon's daughter including her memories of her father.

535. Nicolson, Nigel. *Mary Curzon*. London: Weidenfeld and Nicolson, 1977. 228.

Popular biography of the first Lady Curzon with useful information on, and insights into, her family background and American upbringing, her personality and character, and her relationship with her mother and her husband; makes use of Leiter and Curzon family correspondence and papers.

V. The Press

Curzon's early political career, viceroyalty, return to public office in 1916 and membership in the War Cabinet, and foreign secretaryship are all well documented in the national press in Britain and India. He himself contributed extensively to newspapers such as *The Times* in the form of letters and articles. The following sections note the names and, where known, the political allegiances of contemporary newspapers which throw light on Curzon's career. Curzon took a close interest in press comment and his albums of press cuttings among his papers in the India Office Library and Records include material from most of the following newspapers. They constitute a prime source for contemporary press coverage of Curzon's career. Further details of the politics, ownership, editorship, etc., of the British newspapers below can be found in Chris Cook and Brendan Keith, *British historical facts 1830–1900* (London, 1975) and David Butler and Jennie Freeman, *British political facts 1900–1967* (London, 1968). Copies of the newspapers themselves can be consulted at the British Library's newspaper library at Colindale, London.

536. British newspapers

Daily Chronicle (Liberal)

Daily Express (Independent/Conservative)

Daily Graphic (Independent/Conservative)

Daily Herald (Labour)

Daily Mail (Independent/Conservative)

Daily Mirror (Independent)

Daily News (Radical)

Daily Telegraph (Conservative)

Evening News

Evening Standard

Financial Times (Independent)

Illustrated London News (Independent/Conservative)

Manchester Guardian (Independent/Liberal)

Morning Advertiser (Independent/Conservative)

Morning Herald (Independent)

Morning Post (Conservative)

News of the World (Liberal/Independent)

Observer (Independent/Conservative)

Pall Mall Gazette

The Spectator (Liberal/Radical)

The Standard (Conservative)

Sunday Chronicle

Sunday Herald (Independent conservative)

The Times (Independent/Conservative)

Westminster Gazette (Liberal)

537. Indian newspapers
   Copies of many of the following English-language and native Indian news-papers can be consulted in the India Office Library and Records.

Allahabad Pioneer

Bengalee

Bengal Times

Bombay Gazette

Calcutta Englishman

The East

India

Indian Daily News

Indian Daily Telegraph

Indian Spectator

Kaiser-i-Hind

Madras Mail

Native Opinion

The Pioneer

Rast Goftar

Satya Prahash

Simla News
The Times of India
Tribune

VI. Sound Recordings

The following recordings (538–543) are all held by the BBC Sound Archive, London.

538. Talk by Harold Nicolson on "I knew a man: Lord Curzon of Kedleston" 20 July 1939 (F39/76).

539. References to Curzon in "In search of the past," a series of six reminiscent talks by Harold Nicolson, 12 January–23 February 1955 (AA T30704).

540. References to Curzon by Harold Nicolson in a program on Lord Kitchener, 7 February 1960 (LP25872).

541. Program on Curzon's life and work, 23 March 1955 (21941–42).

542. Childhood memories of Curzon by Rosemary Meynell in "Midland Miscellany," 15 November 1960 (LP26547).

543. References to Curzon in a talk by Evelyn Waugh about the novelist, Alfred Duggan (son of Curzon's second wife), 29 June 1964 (T29701).

The following recordings (544–45) form part of the *Plain Tales From The Raj* collection of tape-recorded interviews in the India Office Library and Records, London.

544. Reminiscences of Sir Gilbert Laithwaite 1919–43, former private secretary to the viceroy, including recollections of Curzon's working habits (MSS Eur R 38/1–4).

545. Reminiscences of her childhood and life in India 1876–1919 of Grace Norie, daughter of the head of the Indian forestry service, including the demonstration of unpopularity against Curzon at the Delhi Durbar in 1903, and Curzon's general arrogance (MSS Eur R 50/1–4).

VII. Visual Representation

A. FILMS

The following films (546–53) are held by the British Film Institute, London.

546. The viceregal procession during the Delhi Durbar of 1902, including Lord and Lady Curzon and the Duke and Duchess of Connaught on "richly caparisoned elephants," accompanied by members of the ruling princely houses of India, also on elephants; followed by Lord Kitchener, the provincial governors and other dignitaries in landaus, 29 December 1902 (Produced by R.W. Paul; location no.: 15941 A(c)).

547. Further scenes from the Delhi Durbar, including the review of troops, the viceroy's party on elephants, etc., 29 December 1902 (Produced by R.W. Paul; location no.: 15941 A(b)).

548. Curzon speaking at the unveiling of a statue of Washington in Trafalgar Square, 4 July 1921 (Pathe Gazette; location no.: 605900A).

549. Curzon and other members of the privy council outside Buckingham Palace on the conclusion of the Irish peace settlement, 8 December 1921 (Topical Film Company; N.1585).

550. Bonar Law, Curzon, and the other members of the Cabinet in 10 Downing Street; thought to be film of the new government after the November 1922 election (Topical Film Company; N.1634).

551. Stanley Baldwin, Sir Robert Horne, Curzon, and others at Chequers, 31 May 1923; entitled "Thinking out his problems" (Topical Film Company; 614–1).

552. Stanley Baldwin, Curzon, Lloyd George, and others in a film entitled "Parliamentary crisis," c. 17–21 January 1924 (Topical Film Company; location no.: 8165 A(c)).

553. Short newsreel item reporting Curzon's death, 23 March 1925 (Topical Film Company; 708–2).

The following films (554–59) are all held in the Visnews Film Library, London.

554. Meeting of representatives of the War Savings Association at the Albert Hall, including film of Curzon's arrival and addresses by Lloyd George and Bonar Law, 25 October 1917 (Gaumont Graphic; no.: V6 R3).

555. The inter-allied conference on the Near East, including film of Curzon, Lloyd George, the Italian, French, and Turkish delegates outside St. James' Palace, 23 February 1921 (Gaumont Graphic; V166 R2).

556. Meeting of dominion premiers at 10 Downing Street, including film of Curzon, Lloyd George, Canadian, Indian, South African, Australian, and other representatives, 7 July 1921 (Gaumont Graphic; V19 R3).

557. Lloyd George, Curzon, and other members of the privy council outside Buckingham Palace on the signing of the Irish peace treaty, 12 December 1921 (Gaumont Graphic; V21 R1).

558. Curzon's last public appearance at the armistice celebrations, 23 March 1925 (Gaumont Graphic; V29 R3).

559. Memorial service to Curzon at Westminster Abbey, 26 March 1925 (Gaumont Graphic; V66 R2).

B. PHOTOGRAPHS

The following list of photographic sources for Curzon's career includes only significant collections of photographs and occasionally single studies where they have become well known as a result of frequent use by biographers, the contemporary press, etc.

The photographs described in entries 560–64 below are all in the India Office Library and Records, London.

560. An extensive collection of photographs among Curzon's own papers, mainly relating to his viceroyalty (the Delhi Durbar, visits to the Persian Gulf and Burma, meetings with Indian princes, frontiers, etc.) but also including his childhood, Oxford, the "Souls," his foreign undersecretaryship, etc. (MSS. Eur. F111–2).

561. Photographs of Curzon in the collection of Colonel George P. Ranken relating to India 1876–1923 (MSS. Eur. F182).

562.   Pictures (c. 62) by Mary Curzon of India and Tibet, in the Cornelia Sorabji collection (MSS. Eur. F165/213).

563.   Album of photographs by General Sir Sydney Muspratt illustrating life in India 1899–1904, including some by Mary Curzon (MSS. Eur. F223/108).

564.   Over forty studies of Curzon and Mary Curzon in India, held by the Department of Prints and Drawings and described in Pauline Rohatgi, *Portraits in the India Office Library and Records*, London, 1983.

565.   Photographs (seven) of Curzon from various sources, mainly as a young M.P. and before his departure for India, in the National Portrait Gallery Archive, London. The Archive holds negatives of five of these (nos.: 31981, 31985, 29096, 29109, 29082).

566.   Two files of photographs of Curzon and Mary Curzon, in the Radio Times Hulton Picture Library, London.

567.   Photograph collection (600 prints, glass negatives, etc.) of James Putnam, confidential private secretary to Curzon in India, illustrating life scenes, personages, inhabitants, buildings, and Curzon's visit to Burma. In the possession of J.J. Putnam Esq., Wood Farm, Blackawton, Totnes, Devon, to whom requests concerning access should be addressed in writing.

C. PORTRAITS

1. Paintings

568.   Curzon as chancellor of Oxford University, 1913, by Philip de Laszlo. In All Soul's College, Oxford. Copies are held by Eton College and the Carlton Club.

569.   Curzon as chancellor of Oxford University, by Sir Hubert von Herkomer. Examination Schools, Oxford University.

570.   Curzon as viceroy, by Sir George Reid. In Government House, Calcutta. Reproduced in *The Sphere*, 22 November 1913.

571.   Curzon as viceroy, by William Logsdail. At Kedleston Hall, Derbyshire.

572.   Portrait by J.S. Sargent. Held by the Royal Geographical Society, London. Copies by A. Hayward and John Cooke are held by the Oriental Club and the National Portrait Gallery respectively.

573.   Watercolor of Curzon c. 1892 by Sir Leslie Ward. Leslie Ward collection, National Portrait Gallery reserve.

574.   The state entry into Delhi 22 December 1902 opening the Durbar, including Curzon and Lady Curzon on the first elephant, followed by the Duke of Connaught and other dignitaries, also on elephants. Sold at Bonham's, 18 June 1981, lot 225.

2. Drawings

575. Curzon on his appointment as under-secretary for foreign affairs 1895, by the Marquess of Granby. Reproduced in the *Review of Reviews*, vol. 12, p. 24.

576. Chalk and charcoal study, by Frank Salisbury, in his sitters' book, 21 March 1921. Salisbury studio sale, 25 September 1985; negative in the National Portrait Gallery (no. 40936).

577. Pen and Indian ink cartoon of Curzon on his appointment as foreign secretary, depicting him on an elephant with foreign dignitaries bowing before him. Sold at Sotheby's 21 November 1973, lot 5, and bought by R.H. Gurney.

578. Series of caricatures of Curzon by Max Beerbohm, including one in 1909 entitled "Once a proconsul, always a proconsul." Published in Rupert Hart-Davis, *A catalogue of the caricatures of Max Beerbohm*, 1972.

579. Ink carbon of Curzon c.1890, by Henry Furniss. National Portrait Gallery no. 3355. Published in *Punch* 22 March 1890, p. 37.

580. Pencil profile September 1924, by Powys Evans. National Portrait Gallery, Evans sketchbooks, box 6.

581. Pen and ink drawing by Powys Evans, undated. Sold at Sotheby's 11 August 1978, lot 36.

582. Ink and watercolor study by Sir F.C. Gould. Victoria and Albert Museum, H.H. Harrod bequest.

583. Cartoons by Sir Bernard Partridge, in *Punch* 8 February 1922 and 16 May 1923.

584. Drawings by Melton Prior of Curzon investing the Maharajah of Cochin, January 1903, and of Curzon's departure (from India?). In the India Office Library and Records.

585. Black and red crayon sketch by William Strang. In the National Gallery, Capetown, South Africa.

D. STATUES

586. Bronze statue by Sir William H. Thorneycroft, erected 1918 outside the Victoria Memorial Hall, Calcutta.

587. Marble statue by F.W. Pomeroy, erected 1912, in the Victoria Memorial Hall, Calcutta.

588. Bronze statue on a stone pedestal by Sir Bertram McKennal, erected in Carlton House Terrace, London, in 1931.

589. Effigies of Curzon and Mary Curzon by Sir Bertram McKennal, at Kedleston Hall.

590. Waxwork of Curzon at Madame Tusaud's, Warwick Castle.

E. PORTRAITS OF CURZON'S FAMILY

591. Portrait of Mary Curzon by Franz Seraph von Lenbach, at Kedleston Hall.

592. Mary Curzon as vicereine by William Logsdail, at Kedleston Hall.

593. Portrait of Grace Curzon by Frank Moss Bennett, 1912, at Kedleston Hall.

594. Portrait of Grace Curzon by Philip de Laszlo, 1916, at Kedleston Hall.

Author Index

The following index excludes published works by Curzon which are arranged alphabetically by title in section 4 above. The index references are to numbered entries and not to pages.

Subject Index

To avoid repetition Curzon has been abbreviated to "C" in the following index.

Lothian, Marquess. *See* Kerr, Philip H.
Lowther, J.W., corresp., 26
Luise, Duchess of Connaught, at the
  Delhi Durbar, 546
Lyttelton, Alfred, papers, 79

Macdonald, Ramsey, 520
Macdonald, Ronald A.B., 6th Baron
  Macdonald, on India, 240
Macdonnell, Sir Antony, 379
Mackail, J.W., 46
Macmillan and Co., corresp. with C, 80
Madras, 60, 93, 132
Madras Mail, 537
Malcolm, Sir Ian Z., 278; papers, 81
Manchester Guardian, 536
mandates, 456
Manners, Henry J.B., Marquess of
  Granby, 7th. Duke of Rutland, draw-
  ing of C, 575
Marcovitch, Lazare, 487
Marker, Col. Raymond J., papers, 82
Matlock, C on, 174
Maurice, J.F., 187
Mekeors monastery, 182
Men's League for Opposing Women's
  Suffrage, C's speech to, 176
Meols, North, C on, 184
Merchant Taylors' School, C's speech to,
  236
Merton College, Oxford, C on, 266
Mesopotamia, 44, 78, 148, 411
Metcalfe, Lady Alexandra, 534
Meynell, Rosemary, 542
Milner, Alfred, Viscount Milner: cor-
  resp., 50, 90, 99; imperialism, 281;
  papers, 83
Minto, Earl of. *See* Elliot-Murray-Kynyn-
  mound, Gilbert J.
Mixed Arbitral Tribunal, 120
Mongolia: C on, 226; Russia and, 207,
  226
Montacute House, C and, 25
Morley, John, Viscount Morley of Black-
  burn, 276, 364; corresp. and memo-
  randa, 33, 54; papers, 84–85
Morning Advertiser, 536
Morning Herald, 536

Morning Post, 536
Mountbatten of Burma, Louis, 1st. Earl
  of, 340
Mount Everest, 84
Muscat, 137
Muspratt, General Sir Sydney, 563
Mysore, 135

Naldera, (?)Alexandra, 396
Napoleon I, Emperor, C on, 201
National Gallery, C and, 25, 194, 197
National League for Opposing Women's
  Suffrage, 4; C and, 468; papers, 1
National Opinion, 537
national service, 76, 78, 90, 448; C and,
  259, 284, 484; papers, 1, 14
Nepal: C and, 420; Maharajah of, 420
Netherlands, The, 43
New Brunswick, 507
Newman, Cardinal John H., 287
News of the World, 536
Nicolson, Sir Harold G., and C, 300–1,
  538–40
Nightingale, Florence, 283
Nile, River, C on, 185
Norie, Grace, on C, 545
North-West Frontier, 15, 36–37, 63, 106,
  167, 231, 366–67, 395, 404
Nushki railway, 36

Observer, 536
Orange, Sir Hugh W., papers, 86
Outlook, The, 292
Oxford University, 205, 560; C as chan-
  cellor, 25, 99, 192, 229a, 250, 266,
  278, 291, 530, 568–69

Palestine, 21, 25, 75, 95, 104, 480
Pall Mall Gazette, 536
Pall Mall Magazine, 179
Palmer, William W., 2nd. Earl of Sel-
  borne, 10, 209, 240; corresp., 75; pa-
  pers, 87
Pamir Mountains, 91, 303; C on, 175,
  212, 231
Pankhurst, Emmeline, 283
Paris, 66; Exhibition (1900), 25, 44, 120;
  Peace Conference, 71, 73, 78, 81,

Serial Publications Index

The following periodicals include both articles about and by Curzon.

About the Author

JAMES G. PARKER has researched extensively in the areas of British and Indian history. He is with the Royal Commission on Historical Manuscripts and has published numerous works, including *The Scots Abroad: Labour, Capital, Enterprise, 1750–1914*.

www.ingramcontent.com/pod-product-compliance
Lightning Source LLC
Chambersburg PA
CBHW030917150426
42812CB00045B/121